# Developing a School Finance System for K–12 Reform in Qatar

Cassandra M. Guarino • Titus Galama • Louay Constant
Gabriella Gonzalez • Jeffery C. Tanner • Charles A. Goldman

Prepared for the Supreme Education Council

RAND
RAND-QATAR POLICY INSTITUTE

The research described in this report was prepared for the Supreme Education Council and conducted within RAND Education and the RAND-Qatar Policy Institute, programs of the RAND Corporation.

**Library of Congress Cataloging-in-Publication Data**

Developing a school finance system for K–12 reform in Qatar / Cassandra M. Guarino ... [et al.].
p. cm.
Includes bibliographical references.
ISBN 978-0-8330-4655-0 (pbk. : alk. paper)
1. Education—Qatar—Finance. 2. Educational change—Qatar.
I. Guarino, Cassandra M.

LB2826.6.Q27D48 2009
379.1'21095363—dc22

2009001425



*Cover design by Eileen Delson La Russo*



Published 2009 by the RAND Corporation
1776 Main Street, P.O. Box 2138, Santa Monica, CA 90407-2138
1200 South Hayes Street, Arlington, VA 22202-5050
4570 Fifth Avenue, Suite 600, Pittsburgh, PA 15213-2665
RAND URL: http://www.rand.org/
To order RAND documents or to obtain additional information, contact
Distribution Services: Telephone: (310) 451-7002;
Fax: (310) 451-6915; Email: order@rand.org

# Preface

In 2001, the leaders of the Arabian Gulf nation of Qatar embarked on a process to reform its K–12 education system. A highlight of that system was the establishment of government-funded Independent schools that operate under a new governance structure and in parallel with Ministry of Education schools. RAND Education worked with Qatar on the design and implementation of the reform, called *Education for a New Era*. This work is reported in a RAND monograph: Dominic Brewer et al., *Education for a New Era: Design and Implementation of K–12 Education Reform in Qatar, MG-548-QATAR.*

In 2004, the Supreme Education Council, in its role as overseer of the reform and of Independent schools, asked RAND to assess the progress and performance of new Independent schools and determine how well the reform is working. One aspect of the assessment was an analysis of school finance relating to the reform efforts. This monograph documents findings from the study and discusses funding and expenditures in the planning and start-up phases of the reform, evaluates the overall effectiveness of the new finance system, and provides modeling tools that can be used to determine funding levels and projected costs in future years. This monograph contains information and analysis of interest not only to the nation of Qatar but also to education policymakers, scholars, and practitioners as well as the wider public elsewhere, in particular in the Gulf States, which share many of the features characteristic of Qatar.

More detailed information about the reform can be found at Qatar's Supreme Education Council Web site: www.education.gov.qa

(Arabic version, with a link to the English version). Further information about the RAND project supporting the reform initiative can be found at www.rand.org/education/.

This project was conducted under the auspices of the RAND Qatar Policy Institute (RQPI) and RAND Corporation's Education unit. RQPI is a partnership of the RAND Corporation and the Qatar Foundation for Education, Science, and Community Development. The aim of RQPI is to offer the RAND style of rigorous and objective analysis to clients in the greater Middle East. In serving clients in the Middle East, RQPI draws on the full professional resources of the RAND Corporation. RAND Education analyzes education policy and practice and supports implementation of improvements at all levels of the education system.

For further information on RQPI, contact the director, Dr. Richard Darilek. He can be reached by email at redar@rand.org; by telephone at +974-492-7400; or by mail at P.O. Box 23644, Doha, Qatar. For more information about RAND Education, contact the associate director, Dr. Charles Goldman. He can be reached by email at charlesg@rand.org; by telephone at +1-310-393-0411, extension 6748; or by mail at RAND, 1776 Main Street, Santa Monica, California 90401 USA.

# Contents

# Figures

# Tables

# Summary

In 2002, reform-minded leaders of Qatar embarked on a sweeping reform of the nation's education system to prepare its people to participate successfully in the global economy. Termed "Education for a New Era," the reform established a new governing body, the Supreme Education Council (SEC), which was to operate independently of the existing Ministry of Education and carry out the various reform measures. The reform design called for some Ministry public schools to be converted to so-called "Independent schools" under the direction of the SEC to encourage key principles of autonomy, accountability, variety, and choice. In addition to the establishment of these new schools, national curriculum standards and assessments were developed to promote and monitor educational progress. After an initial planning phase, 12 Independent schools opened in the 2004–2005 academic year, and 21 more opened in 2005–2006. Growth in the number of Independent schools has continued, with 46 Independent schools serving 18 percent of Qatar's K–12 population in 2006–2007.

RAND worked with Qatar's leaders and the SEC to develop the reform plan and help implement it (Brewer et al., 2007). Following the initial implementation phase, the SEC asked RAND to analyze the progress made by the new school system, including an evaluation of the finance system developed to support the reform. This monograph documents RAND's evaluation of the finance system, and a forthcoming companion report will address other aspects of the reform.

## Study Questions and Approach

This analysis aims to describe and evaluate the evolution of the finance system designed to support the reform in its early stages—specifically, from 2004 to 2006. We examine resource allocation patterns over this time period, develop a set of objectives and analytic tools for evaluating the system, evaluate the system in its early stages of development, and offer suggestions for improving the system. Thus, the monograph addresses the following research questions:

- How have financial resources in the reform been allocated over time?
  - in the reform as a whole
  - in Independent schools
- To what extent does the system of financial support for the reform meet the objectives of a strong school finance system?
- What analytic methods and tools will further the SEC's ability to monitor and modify financial flows to the reform?
- How can the finance system be improved?

We relied on several data sources to assess financial aspects of the reform, including financial data from each Independent school, school administrative data, student-level data and test scores, and information about each student's parents and family life. Our assessment reflects trends from the 2003–2004 planning phase, the first year of school operations in 2004–2005, and the second year of school operations in 2005–2006.

In evaluating the education finance system, we endeavored to understand how financial resources were allocated over time in the reform as a whole and in detail within the Independent school system. Likewise, we sought to ascertain the extent to which the new school finance system supported the growth of the reform and to highlight ways it could be improved.

We developed a framework for evaluating the school finance system, based on its ability to meet six main objectives: adequacy, efficiency, equity, accountability, transparency, and an appropriate balance between stability and responsiveness. We then assessed the system in light of these objectives, developing analytic methods where needed.

## Findings

In assessing trends in resource allocation, we found that total spending on the reform rose from QR 144 million in the start-up phase to QR 523 million in the first year of school operations and to QR 841 million in the second year.[1] Over that time, total spending on operating Independent schools alone more than doubled, from just under QR 200 million to just over QR 400 million as the number of Independent schools rose from 12 to 33.

We found that Independent school operators were hesitant to spend in their first year of operations and carried sizable surpluses of about 15 percent of revenues, on average. In their second year of operation, they spent more but still carried surpluses of about 10 percent of revenues, on average. Some of this hesitancy in spending may have stemmed from general uncertainty regarding funding policies, leading school operators to maintain financial buffers. Some may also have been due to an initial lack of experience in the management of budgets or to a lack of familiarity with the full range of resources that could be purchased by schools.

To assess financial *adequacy*, we investigated whether the reform supplied enough funding to support educational excellence, using a "successful schools" approach. This approach identifies high-performing schools using statistical techniques and calculates average costs in these schools to determine adequate funding levels. Our application of the successful schools approach used 2006 standardized student test scores, regression adjusted for the prior performance, and demographic characteristics of students to rank schools by performance. Adjusted test scores are preferable to average test scores in determining the value a school provides to its pupils in a given year because they help distin-

[1] The Qatari riyal (QR) was approximately equivalent to 0.275 U.S. dollars during the 2004–2006 period, and the exchange rate has remained relatively stable.

guish the school's effect on learning from the performance that would be expected given the abilities of the students who attend the school.

Our adequacy analysis using the successful schools approach showed that higher test scores were associated with higher per-pupil spending, lower per-pupil surpluses, and lower pupil-teacher ratios in the 20 Independent schools examined at the primary school level. Differences in spending, surpluses, and pupil-teacher ratios between the top-performing (based on adjusted student test scores) and bottom 50 percent of primary schools are statistically significant. Top-performing, as well as other schools, received funding adequate to cover their expenditures.

Still, it is too early to establish whether reform schools are receiving adequate funding. First, it is not possible to assert that top-performing schools are "successful schools," unless it is known that these schools are achieving desired levels of learning. Thus, this method ultimately relies on the existence of school performance standards, and these have not yet been established by the SEC. Although we can distinguish better from worse performing schools, the absence of a standard of excellence makes it unclear whether funding is adequate to promote excellence. Second, with so few schools in the sample, we are cautious in regarding our results as evidence of a causal link between resources and performance. The analysis did not reveal a statistically significant relationship between expenditures and student test scores for preparatory and secondary schools, but we do not know if this is due to a lack of association between test scores and financial resources for these schools or because the number of schools is too small to detect a relationship. As the reform grows and more Independent schools are established, additional data will become available for future analysis, improving inference that can be drawn.

In studying financial *efficiency*, we tried to establish whether the reform provides effective educational models at the most economical price. At this point in time, however, it is not yet feasible to determine efficiency because, as noted above, standards for excellence have not been defined. Once they are established, it should be possible to identify which schools are successful and to compare resource use and teaching practices among them to determine which ones are most efficient. By supplementing the quantitative analyses described above with a case study approach to examine the operations and teaching practices of successful schools, it will be possible to uncover factors that might yield high achievement at the lowest cost.

Our assessment of *equity* in the reform employs a comparison of resource use in boys' and girls' schools. We found that boys' and girls' schools had similar levels of resources and spending, but that this apparent similarity masked significant differences in cost structure. The most salient factor in decomposing these cost structures is the gender and nationality of teachers in Independent schools. Male teachers earn around QR 5,585 more than females per month, and Qataris earn approximately the same monthly premium over non-Qataris. Female Qatari teachers earn approximately the same monthly salary as male non-Qataris, and male Qatari teachers earn well over twice the monthly wage of female non-Qatari teachers. By cultural convention, preparatory and secondary school students as well as primary-school girls have teachers of the same gender, whereas primary school boys can be taught by either gender. As a result, boys' schools generally employ male teachers who cost more. However, because male Qataris generally do not enter the teaching profession, the boys' schools offset this higher cost by employing more than five times as many non-Qatari male teachers as Qatari male teachers. In contrast, girls' schools had a nearly equal number of Qatari and non-Qatari teachers. The gender and nationality factors roughly offset each other to produce a similar overall spending pattern. Despite the apparent gender equity in school funding, the underlying differences in the gender and nationality of the teacher populations imply that the balance is tenuous and depends on maintaining a particular labor force composition. For example, increasing the share of Qataris employed in Independent schools, as desired by the government and promoted through a set of governmental policies involving target quotas termed "Qatarization," could have a differential effect on boys' and girls' schools.

We developed a flexible forecasting tool to investigate the potential effect of various policy changes, such as Qatarization, on total reform expenditures. In one such scenario, we found that some schools stood to gain significantly but others had much to lose under enforcement of Qatarization target quotas and compensatory adjustments to funding would alter the gender balance. As a result, the enforcement of Qatarization policies could affect funding equity across boys' and girls' schools as well as conflict with the goal of improving student achievement.

Two primary mechanisms are used in the finance system to promote accountability to ensure that recipients of public funds produce high-quality education: fiscal oversight and school choice. The fiscal oversight mechanism involves regulating school spending and the labor market for school personnel. We found that the reform relied on this type of oversight as the primary mechanism to ensure accountability, as evidenced by several initial and added regulatory provisions. In the period covered by our analysis, the SEC reduced funding sources and froze surpluses to prevent the misuse of surplus funds. Although these restrictions appear to have achieved their desired fiscal effect, it is unclear whether they have provided incentives for schools to strive for improved performance. In addition, the second accountability mechanism, parental choice, is only partially effective in providing incentives for Independent schools to raise achievement, as capacity constraints make it difficult for them to accept new students. Without the incentive to attract students, the choice mechanism provides little incentive to raise performance.

The principle of *transparency* was meant to be manifest in the reform's data systems. These systems were designed to produce needed information for monitoring and analysis, as evidenced by a comprehensive set of financial reporting forms that schools are required to fill out and submit. However, we discovered areas of concern within the system during the time period covered by our evaluation, including nonelectronic data storage, inconsistent time periods for school statements reducing comparability across schools, nonstandard categorizations of expenses, and a lack of unique staff identifiers. The lack of these standards made analytical work difficult in some areas. A new electronic management information system has been partially implemented since our analysis was conducted. It is hoped that the new system will eventually alleviate many of these problems.

A final objective of a sound education finance system is striking a balance between *stability* and *responsiveness*. Stability refers to a predictable operating environment that allows school operators to establish both long- and short-term strategies for improving their schools; responsiveness indicates an ability of the governing body to intervene and fine-tune the reform to improve its functioning. Our findings indicate that the SEC emphasized responsiveness over stability in the years covered by this analysis. The SEC responded to information on school surpluses with numerous changes in financial policies. For instance, schools were changed from for-profit to nonprofit entities, surpluses were placed in holding accounts, operator salaries were capped, grant funding was discontinued, and start-up funds were capped. Still other changes in regulations stemmed from national goals, particularly goals meant to promote the employment of Qataris and increase Qatari base salaries by 40 percent. As a result of the many swift and strong policy changes over the first two years of operation of Independent schools, the system has lacked stability. This uncertainty likely made it difficult for school operators to plan for the long term and make the kinds of investments in quality that would eventually use the full per-pupil allotment. Furthermore, some of the policy changes implemented ran counter to the reform principals of autonomy, accountability, variety, and choice. It is understandable, however, that a new system might undergo widespread change in its initial stages. Perhaps, moving forward, the system will achieve a greater degree of stability.

## Conclusions and Recommendations

Qatar's K–12 education reform has made notable progress in a few short years. It has founded a growing set of new schools and established a comprehensive infrastructure for financial support and monitoring. With a rich array of financial reports and consecutive years of similar test-score data, it is now possible to develop new measures of financial and educational performance, analyze trends and differences across institutions and time periods, and forecast spending projections under various policy scenarios. In this monograph, we have explored the wealth of data available and pointed the way to analyses that can inform the SEC in future decisionmaking. We also developed a flexible forecasting tool that serves both in evaluating current flows of revenues and expenditures and in assessing the effect of proposed policy changes.

Our assessment revealed areas for improvement in the finance system to enrich its capacity to support the reform and its overall mission. We offer the following recommendations:

- To determine levels of funding adequate to support educational excellence, we recommend continued analysis using a successful schools approach along the lines of the one we describe and implement in our study. As the reform expands and performance targets that represent excellence in achievement are established, this methodology will yield increasingly useful information.
- To obtain information that would lead to greater efficiency in school operations, we recommend supplementing the quantitative analyses described above with a case study approach to examine the operations and teaching practices of successful schools and uncover factors that might yield high achievement at the lowest cost.
- To address potential equity issues, we recommend that policies with different effects on different types of schools be investigated before implementation, using a forecasting model such as the one we have developed.
- To improve transparency, we recommend that the new information system include improved longitudinal tracking mechanisms as well as introduce more uniform categorization of personnel and expenditures. The current reporting system is in the process of being replaced by a management information system; its design provides an opportunity to address the data issues identified in this study.
- To strengthen accountability for school quality, we recommend an expansion of the choice mechanism through increases in capacity where possible to strengthen the system's ability to hold schools accountable for providing high-quality instruction.

- To improve stability, we recommend that, going forward, the pace of policy change be slowed to allow school operators to assess long-term prospects and plan for multiyear investments in resources that may improve educational quality.

In summary, we have evaluated the school finance system developed to implement Qatar's K–12 education reform in its early years. In so doing, we have devised a set of analytic methods and tools and suggested a number of potential improvements. It is hoped that these analyses, tools, and suggestions will be useful to the SEC as the reform expands and that they will also provide helpful information to other nations embarking on education reforms, particularly those in regions that face contextual issues similar to those in Qatar.

# Acknowledgments

We thank the SEC's Education Institute, Evaluation Institute, and Shared Services Department for their assistance in obtaining critical study data. Her Excellency Sheikha Ahmad Al Mahmoud, Ms. Sabah Al Haidoos, Mr. Adel Al Sayed, and Mr. Tariq Al Abdulla assisted us by cooperating throughout the study and by sharing their perspectives on preliminary findings. Dr. Nafez Alyan, Mr. Saleh Mohammed Al Khulaifi, Mr. Adnan Jabir, and Ms. Nadia Baker of the Education Institute's Finance Office, and Mr. Jacob Abraham and Ms. Reem Al-Binali of the Shared Services Department assisted us by providing data and guidance in interpreting the data.

On the RAND team, we thank Abdulrazaq Al-Kurawi for valuable input and liaison support in Doha; Rita Karam, Teresa Taningco, Reham Malik, Michelle Cho, and Anga Timilsina for assistance with research and analysis; Reham Badr El-Din Sayed and Kayla Ferguson for help with the translation of data from Arabic to English; Chris Fitzmartin for managing access to the Qatar National Educational Database System; Reham El-Din Sayed, Chris Dirks, and Lawrence Tingson for the high-quality administrative support they provided; and Cathleen Stasz, Catherine Augustine, Dominic Brewer, and Paco Martorell for their very helpful reviews.

# Abbreviations

| | |
|---|---|
| HEI | Higher Education Institute |
| LLC | Limited Liability Corporation |
| LOSS | lowest obtainable scale score |
| OPEC | Organization of the Petroleum Exporting Countries |
| QCEA | Qatar Comprehensive Educational Assessment |
| QCSS | Qatar Comprehensive Schooling Surveys |
| QNEDS | Qatar National Educational Database System |
| QR | Qatari riyal |
| SEC | Supreme Education Council |
| SSO | School Support Organization |

CHAPTER ONE

# Introduction

Education is a critical component of any nation's effort to prepare its youth for civic participation and a global economy. The leaders of the Arabian Gulf nation of Qatar view education as the key to Qatar's economic and social progress. Long concerned that the country's education system was not producing high-quality outcomes and was rigid, outdated, and resistant to reform, Qatari leaders approached the RAND Corporation in 2001, asking it to examine the kindergarten through grade 12 (K–12) education system in Qatar and to recommend options for building a world-class system consistent with other Qatari initiatives for social and political change. After selecting the options that seemed best suited to the Qatar context, the Emir of Qatar issued Decree No. 37 in 2002, which established a Supreme Education Council (SEC) as the highest authority in Qatar's education sector to lead a reform entitled *Education for a New Era*. Much of the reform focused on K–12 education and was designed to decentralize authority and increase flexibility based on the principles of autonomy, accountability, variety, and choice.

The K–12 reform design embodied three primary levers for change to the existing school system. First, "Independent schools" were established in the form of charter schools that were operated independently from the existing Ministry of Education (hereafter referred to as the Ministry). School operators were allowed to exercise autonomy over both academic matters—such as mission, curriculum, and pedagogy—and financial matters—such as staffing and resource allocation. This autonomy was intended to lead to variety, which in turn would lead to quality improvements in schooling options. Parents were permitted to exercise a limited degree of choice over their children's enrollment. All Independent schools were converted from preexisting Ministry schools, although many were located in new facilities. Twelve Independent schools opened in the 2004–2005 academic year, 21 more in 2005–2006, and 13 in 2006–2007. Thus, in 2006–2007, 46 Independent schools were operating alongside approximately 164 Ministry schools and 292 private schools. Independent school students represented approximately 18 percent of all K–12 students in Qatar, both private and public in that year. The number of Independent schools has continued to grow, with 19 more opening in 2007–2008 and 15 more opening in 2008–2009.

A second important lever for change was the development of new curriculum standards for Independent schools. These were developed with the assistance of outside contractors and covered four subjects—Arabic, English, mathematics, and science—and they were benchmarked to international standards.

Third, standardized national assessments were developed and administered in the same four subjects to students in publicly funded schools to determine how well they met the new standards. May 2007 marked the third administration of standards-based assessments to government-sponsored schools in Qatar.[1]

After the decree, Qatari leaders asked RAND to analyze and support implementation of the reform. This monograph focuses on RAND's evaluation of the finance system that was established to support the reform during the 2003–2004 planning phase and the first two years of operation of Independent schools—2004–2005 and 2005–2006.[2] Our overall assessment of the system employs a conceptual framework based on generally recognized objectives of school finance systems:

---

[1] Independent, Ministry, and private Arabic schools were assessed in 2005 and 2006 but only Independent schools were assessed in 2007.

[2] This report focuses on these two years. The earliest phases of the K–12 school reform effort—i.e., those before 2004–2005—are documented in Brewer et al. (2007). More detailed information about the reform can be found at Qatar's Supreme Education Council Web site. Further information about the RAND project supporting the reform initiative can be found on the RAND Education Web site.

transparency, equity, adequacy, efficiency, accountability, stability, and responsiveness.

Data for the study consisted of financial reports and audited statements furnished by the SEC's Office of Finance and Office of Shared Services. The purpose of the RAND analysis was to describe the evolution of financial trends and resource allocation patterns in the early years of the reform, develop a set of objectives and analytic tools for evaluating the finance system designed to support the reform, evaluate the system in its early stages of development, and offer suggestions for improving the system. Thus, this report addresses the following research questions:

- How have financial resources in the reform been allocated over time?
  - in the reform as a whole
  - in Independent schools
- To what extent does the system of financial support for the reform meet the objectives of a strong school finance system?
- What analytic methods and tools will further the SEC's ability to monitor and modify financial flows to the reform?
- How can the finance system be improved?

## Qatar Context

Qatar is one of the smallest Gulf states—only 11,427 sq km—but significant oil and natural gas reserves, along with its strategic location and progressive leaders, give it a unique status in today's world. Qatar is one of the world's wealthiest countries, and its economy has grown dramatically over the past decades. The Organization of the Petroleum Exporting Countries (OPEC), of which Qatar is a member, reports that Qatar's gross domestic product per capita in 2007 was $75,426 (Organization of the Petroleum Exporting Countries, 2008).[3]

Several features of labor markets in Qatar and other Gulf nations have important implications for school finance. Qatar imports much

[3] This figure would likely be much higher if it were to include only Qatari nationals.

of the labor needed for its economy, especially in the private and semiprivate sectors. In-country sources estimate the 2006 population in Qatar at 1.04 million (Qatar General Secretariat, 2008, Table 5). The nation does not publish figures for the total Qatari and non-Qatari (or expatriate) population, but using figures for the population ages 15 and above, estimates are that Qataris constitute about 18 percent of the population (Qatar General Secretariat, 2008, Table 20). The balance is composed of expatriate workers and, in some cases, their families.

Concurrent with education reform, a national policy to promote the participation of Qatari citizens in the labor force—termed "Qatarization"—has been a high priority of the country's current leaders. Qatarization is a form of affirmative action that has relied primarily on the use of quotas to induce employers to hire Qatari nationals. It aims to develop the skills of the Qatari workforce through employment, education, and training. Private and semiprivate or parastatal corporations, such as Qatar Petroleum, have been primary targets of the quota system, but the school system has also been charged with promoting the employment of Qataris. Sanctions for failing to meet Qatarization quotas have as yet been minimal—and often involve mandates to spend money on training Qataris—but pressures to comply continue to mount. The increased participation of Qataris in the workforce, if realized, has important implications for the school finance system, since Qataris earn higher salaries than expatriate workers of similar education and experience. Thus far, however, these quotas have not been rigorously enforced, and many schools fall short of targets (Stasz et al., 2007).

Along with Qatarization, gender-related features of the Qatari labor market play an important role. Schools are segregated by gender. Female teachers may teach girls at all levels and boys at the primary school level (grades 1–6). Male teachers may teach only boys. In addition, men and women do not generally work together in the same institution, so, for example, a boys' primary school with female teachers is likely to have an all female staff. Traditionally, in the Qatari labor force, men earn higher salaries than do women, largely because of a different benefit structure.[4] As a result, employees generally do not expect gender parity in compensation. In addition, a degree of occupational segregation by gender exists within the labor market, as in many other countries. Women are far more likely to become teachers than men are, and few male Qataris enter the teaching profession. Given that only male teachers are employed in boys' preparatory (grades 7–9) and secondary (grades 10–12) schools, many male expatriate teachers must be brought in to teach boys. Thus, the proportion of expatriate male teachers is greater than that of expatriate female teachers. As we discuss below, salary disparities between men and women and between Qataris and non-Qataris have a differential effect on finances across schools of different levels and genders.[5]

## Implications of the Qatar Experience for School Finance Systems in Other Countries

Setting up a finance system to support education reform in Qatar has been a large undertaking requiring the establishment of new funding structures and reporting systems. The Qatar experience provides useful lessons that can be applied elsewhere. Other countries embarking on ambitious educational restructuring can gain valuable knowledge by studying the growth experiences of Qatar's new school finance system. Countries in the Gulf region, in particular, share many of the distinctive features of the Qatar context, such as gender-segregated schools, gender-differentiated salary structures, and policies such as Qatarization designed to promote the employment of citizens (Gonzalez et al., 2008).

In addition to lessons learned, this monograph provides a set of guidelines for analyzing and predicting educational expenditures

---

[4] Several traditional types of "allowances" are attached to salaries in Qatar, which may include separate payments for social needs, housing, and transportation, for example. Men and women differ in their eligibility for these allowances.

[5] See Brewer et al. (2007) and Stasz et al. (2007) for more general background on Qatar and these issues (Qatarization and gender segregation in the labor market) in particular.

that can be applied to school systems in many nations. The evaluation framework developed in the study easily translates to other school finance contexts.

## Limitations of the Study

The education reform investigated in this monograph is in its initial stages and is still evolving. Findings relating to the planning, start-up, and first and second years of operation of Independent schools may not be representative of the system in subsequent years of operation.

In addition, we have relied on data made available to us. As discussed in detail in later chapters, not all data were available at a level of detail or completeness that might be most informative. Therefore, certain analyses were based on assumptions and judgments regarding the appropriate way to use the information. In these cases, we explain the assumptions and decision rules used.

We have also developed a methodology for determining adequate funding levels in Independent schools. Given that data were available for only a few schools, our findings are limited. As the reform grows, this methodology will provide more definitive information.

## Organization of the Monograph

Chapter Two presents an overview and analysis of trends in expenditures and resource allocation in Qatar's K–12 education reform. Chapter Three outlines and implements a framework for evaluating the reform's finance system against a set of objectives. Chapter Four provides a forecasting tool that projects expenditures on the reform at different levels of aggregation into the future under different possible scenarios. Chapter Five summarizes findings and recommendations for improvements within the system. Data analysis methods are discussed in each chapter along with our findings. In addition, the monograph contains two appendixes: Appendix A provides detailed descriptions of the data used in the analyses and Appendix B lays out the baseline assumptions used in our forecasting model.

CHAPTER TWO

# Trends in Financial Resource Allocation in the Reform

In this chapter, we present trends in expenditures and resource allocation throughout the system to help us understand how and why spending changed over time in the initial years of the reform. The first part of this chapter documents total spending on the reform, categorized as funds flowing to the various schools, institutes, offices, and contractors associated with the reform. The second part examines revenues and expenditures, including staff expenditures, across the first two cohorts of Independent schools. The information provided in this chapter serves three purposes. It addresses our first research question regarding resource allocation in the reform as a whole and in Independent schools. Second, it provides background information for our evaluation of the finance system discussed in the next chapter. Finally, it serves as the foundation for the information used to build our forecasting model presented in Chapter Four.

## Total Spending on the Reform

In documenting total spending on the reform, we present an overall picture of costs during three initial periods:[1]

[1] Spending on the reform actually began in the 2002–2003 fiscal year but this year was excluded from the analysis because expenditures were not accurately recorded during that period and many expenditures were missing. The first year for which we examine data is the

1. planning phase (April 2003–March 2004)
2. start-up and first year of Independent school operation (April 2004–March 2005)
3. second year of Independent school operation (April 2005–March 2006).

The information presented was derived from reports provided by the Office of Shared Services—the office charged with managing the budgets for the SEC and allocating funds to the various offices, institutes, and schools involved in the reform. The data sources are described in detail in Appendix A.[2] The monetary amounts reported in this study are in Qatari riyals (QR). Readers may wish to translate these into more familiar currencies, such as U.S. dollars or British pounds. Generally, over the time period covered in the study, the exchange rates were 3.64 QR per one U.S. dollar and 7.0 QR per one British pound.[3]

Figure 2.1 illustrates total spending on the various components of the reform—Independent schools, Institutes (the Education,[4] Higher

---

2003–2004 fiscal year. Beginning with 2003–2004 thus allows us to examine spending for an entire fiscal year and to make more appropriate comparisons across years.

2 Note that the data presented here cover the fiscal year used by the Office of Shared Services, which runs from April 1 to March 31, whereas Independent schools operate on the academic cycle from September 1 to August 31. The data presented here thus do not coincide with the exact period of the planning and operation phases of Independent schools. In some cases, the periods covered by the different sources of data varied from one year to the next and sometimes overlapped. For example, in 2004–2005, we have one spreadsheet dated April 1–July 15 and another dated April 1–March 31. We therefore made some assumptions in determining and separating the costs over the three periods. These assumptions are described in Appendix A.

3 The Qatari riyal is pegged to the U.S. dollar but fluctuates significantly with respect to the British pound. As of August 6, 2007, one QR = 0.135 British pound.

4 The Education Institute contracts with and overseas Independent schools and provides them with the financial, professional development, and other resources necessary to educate K–12 students successfully. It also develops curriculum standards and interfaces with the Evaluation Institute in the translation of standards into testing measures.

**Figure 2.1**
**Total Spending on the Reform from April 1, 2003, Through March 31, 2006**

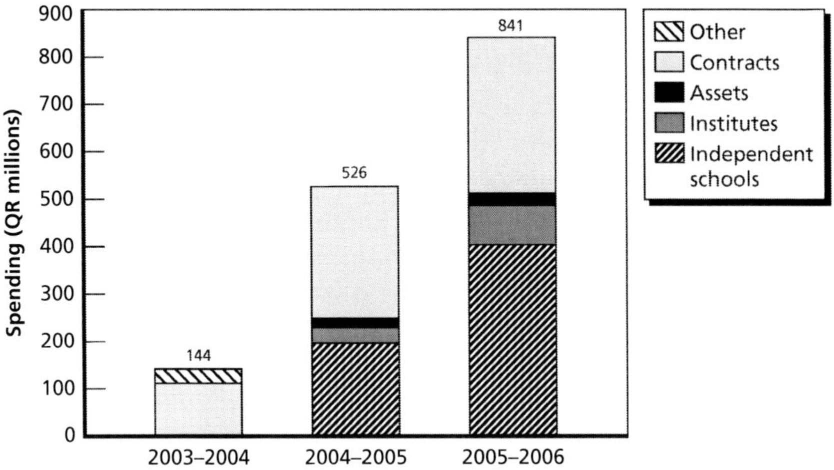


SOURCE: Office of Shared Services: total reform expenditures.
RAND *MG839-2.1*

Education,[5] and Evaluation[6] Institutes, the Office of Shared Services, and the Office of Communications), assets, contracts, and other expenses. The first bar shows the spending in the planning phase of the reform, the second bar the start-up and first year of Independent school operation, and the third bar the second year of Independent school operation.

---

[5] The Higher Education Institute provides postsecondary career counseling, assesses and certifies the quality of postsecondary institutions, and administers new scholarship programs for students to study in postsecondary institutes worldwide. We considered removing Higher Education Institute costs from total costs, since our analysis focuses mainly on costs associated with operating or overseeing Independent schools. However, for the periods April 2004 to March 2005 and April 2005 to July 2005, we are unable to distinguish spending on the Higher Education Institute from that on the other institutes and departments under the auspices of the Supreme Education Council. We include the Higher Education Institute in the assessment of total costs to allow comparisons across time. Costs associated with the Higher Education Institute are available for the period July 2006 to March 2006 and totaled 16 percent of total costs of all institutes and departments. These data are shown in Figure 2.2.

[6] The Evaluation Institute is in charge of the standardized assessments that measure the performance of schools, students, and other education constituents.

It is important to note that expenditures on the reform are accompanied by savings within the Ministry of Education system, because all Independent schools were converted from Ministry schools. Therefore, from the point of view of the entire Qatar education system, reform expenditures may not result in added overall costs. We do not track expenditures in Ministry schools, however, and cannot offer information on overall educational "costs" in the country at the current time. Data on total expenditures in the Ministry are published annually in its Annual Statistics Report. Before the K–12 reform was announced in 2002, the Ministry reported total spending of 1.61 billion QR on K–12 education (nominal QR), which corresponds to 22,249 QR on a per-pupil basis, for the 2001–2002 school year (Ministry of Education, 2005). After the reform was established, it became difficult to rely on reports of total Ministry spending, because certain reform expenditures related to Independent school staffing were carried along in the reported Ministry totals. We are unable to distinguish these expenditures from others within the Ministry reports and thus cannot provide a side-by-side comparison of Ministry and reform-related spending.

Figure 2.1 shows that, during the planning phase, expenditures on the reform totaled around QR 144 million (nominal QR). Approximately 80 percent of total spending was on external contracts. Contracts accounted for a large share of expenditures in this phase, as contractors were brought in to provide expertise not available in Qatar at the time. Contractors were initially responsible for developing the infrastructure for the reform (for example, developing curriculum standards and national assessments), hiring and training local staff to eventually manage the reform, and reporting on progress to the SEC. As the infrastructure grew and Independent schools were brought into operation, the share of the reform budget devoted to contractors diminished.[7]

Contracts were issued to various organizations for various purposes. In the planning phase, the two largest contractors were the

[7] The 2003–2004 data are based on an itemized list of payments made by the Ministry of Finance on behalf of the SEC and are not readily comparable with the April 2004–March 2006 data. We identified contracts for 2003–2004 by going through each payment on the itemized list, but we were unable to map payments to the exact categories in the 2004–2005 and 2005–2006 years.

National Opinion Research Center—tasked with designing and implementing the Qatar National Education Database System (QNEDS)—and RAND Corporation—tasked with overseeing the implementation of the Qatar K–12 reform design. Each contractor received more than QR 5 million between April 2003 and March 2004, although the actual amounts are difficult to specify from the documentation. As schools came into operation, contractors were brought in to help train school administrators and teachers. These organizations, referred to as School Support Organizations (SSOs),[8] were Mosaica, Multiserve, and the Centre for British Teachers. In addition to these organizations, other contractors, such as the German Technical Cooperation, the Academy for Educational Development, the Queensland government, Arab Educational Services, and the College of the North Atlantic, were hired to supplement the activities of the other contractors and help with training and the development of national standards and curricula. We received records of spending on some of these contracts, but it was difficult to break these down accurately into amounts spent per type of contract per fiscal year, because information on certain contracts was missing and the information covered differing contractual periods. Our best estimate of SSO support amounted to approximately QR 44 million to the first cohort of 12 Independent schools and approximately QR 54 million to the second cohort of 21 schools from February 2004 to July 2006.

Total spending during the start-up and first year of Independent school operation amounted to around QR 526 million. During this phase, funding for the institutes that make up the administrative infrastructure of the reform represented approximately 7 percent of total spending, and assets procurement represented 4 percent. The greatest share of spending, at just over half, remained on contracts, but funding to Independent schools made up a significant portion, at 37 percent. Funding to the schools included start-up funds and funds designated

[8] SSOs were hired under contract to provide a variety of services to schools, including professional development, curriculum development, and budget management. SSOs worked with a school or a group of schools for 18 months: six months before the start of the school year and then 12 months during the operation of the school. Schools were eligible for SSO support only in their first year of operation.

for operational expenditures but not the in-kind support in the form of SSOs or other types of professional development that were instead funded through contracts.

The third phase included the second year of operation for the first group of Independent schools and the establishment of the second group. In this phase, total spending grew to approximately QR 841 million. Spending on Independent schools as a share of total spending increased from about 37 to about 48 percent. Although the share of total spending devoted to asset procurement remained the same, the share devoted to institute operations increased slightly, from 7 to 9 percent. The share of spending on external contracts continued to decline, which was expected as the oversight institutions and Independent schools developed the capacity to manage their own operations. Contracts remained a significant share of the budget, however, at 39 percent.

Figure 2.2 illustrates how resources were allocated within and across the institutes and the SEC Offices of Shared Services and Communications from July 16, 2005, through March, 21, 2006—the most recent year for which we have such data.[9] In the figure, general and administrative expenses include such items as operations and administration, professional charges, and travel. Note that these figures do not include operational funding within Independent schools. Also note that allocations to the Higher Education Institute (HEI) represent approximately 16 percent of the total amount in this period. As noted above, we were unable to separate HEI expenditures from other expenditures across all three periods represented in Figure 2.1. We therefore included HEI expenditures in the totals reported.

The largest share of spending by the institutes was on contracts and project expenses. Spending on contracts was particularly high in the Evaluation Institute, which develops and administers both the Qatar Comprehensive Educational Assessment (QCEA) and the Qatar

[9] We present this information for one year only because time periods covered in the spreadsheets differed between 2004–2005 and 2005–2006, reducing comparability over time.

**Figure 2.2**
**Resource Allocation Within and Across Institutes and SEC Offices from July 16, 2005, Through March 31, 2006**

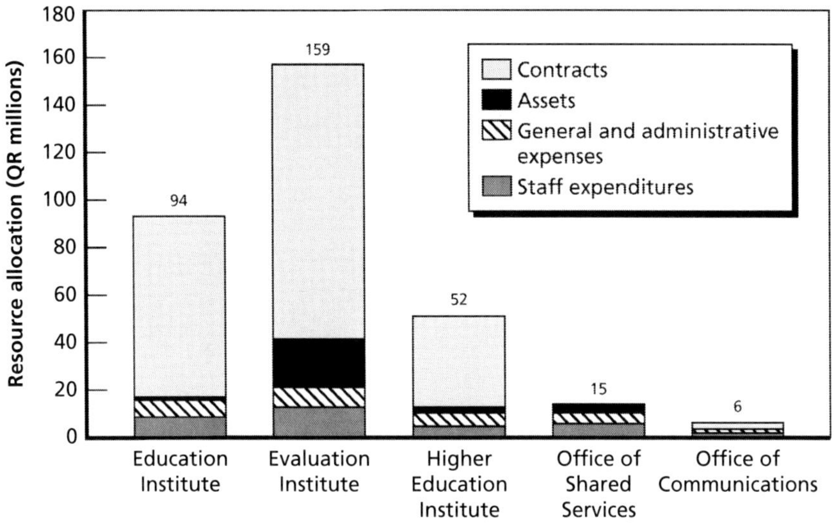


SOURCE: Office of Shared Services: operational expenditures on institutes.
RAND *MG839-2.2*

Comprehensive Schooling Surveys (QCSS) and warehouses the QNEDS. The Evaluation Institute also allocates more resources to its fixed assets and loans than the other institutes do, and these are most likely associated with the infrastructure needed to develop, administer, and store the results of the assessments and surveys.

## Spending on Independent Schools in 2004–2005 and 2005–2006

The first Independent schools—opened in the 2004–2005 academic year—are referred to as "Generation I" schools and those that opened in subsequent years are referred to as "Generation II," "Generation III," etc. A profile of the first two generations of schools, broken out by grade level, school gender, size, and year is provided in Table 2.1 using data provided by the Finance Office in the form of audited statements,

**Table 2.1**
**Generation I and Generation II Independent Schools**

| | Generation I 2004–2005 | | | Generation I 2005–2006 | | | Generation II 2005-2006 | | |
|---|---|---|---|---|---|---|---|---|---|
| School Type | No. of Schools | Students | Average Students/ School | No. of Schools | Students | Average Students/ School | No. of Schools | Students | Average Students/ School |
| Primary model boys | 0 | 0 | N/A | 0 | 0 | N/A | 3 | 1,573 | 524.3 |
| Primary boys | 3 | 1,666 | 555.3 | 3 | 1,866 | 622.0 | 1 | 625 | 625.0 |
| Primary girls | 4 | 2,691 | 672.8 | 4 | 2,717 | 679.3 | 7 | 3,971 | 567.3 |
| Preparatory boys | 2 | 1,201 | 600.5 | 2 | 1,271 | 635.5 | 2 | 1,240 | 620.0 |
| Preparatory girls | 0 | 0 | N/A | 0 | 0 | N/A | 4 | 2,232 | 558.0 |
| Secondary boys | 1 | 245 | 245.0 | 1 | 348 | 348.0 | 2 | 1,224 | 612.0 |
| Secondary girls | 0 | 0 | N/A | 0 | 0 | N/A | 2 | 948 | 474.0 |
| Complexes boys | 1 | 1,790 | 1,790.0 | 1 | 1,860 | 1,860.0 | 0 | 0 | N/A |
| Complexes girls | 1 | 1,524 | 1,524.0 | 1 | 2,163 | 2,163.0 | 0 | 0 | N/A |
| Total | 12 | 9,117 | 759.8 | 12 | 10,225 | 852.1 | 21 | 11,813 | 562.5 |

SOURCE: Finance Office.

NOTE: N/A = not applicable.

cash flow statements, staffing reports, and Finance Office data on student enrollment. Primary schools include regular and "model" schools. Model schools are primary schools for boys that are taught by women.[10] Other boys' primary schools are taught by men. Boys who attend model schools typically have a one- or two-year transition in a male-taught primary school before they enter preparatory school. The largest Independent schools are "complexes," which are schools that span a number of grades from kindergarten through grade 12.

Most Independent schools were primary schools and Generation I schools—with an average enrollment of 760 students in 2004–2005 and 852 students in 2005–2006—tended to be larger than those in Generation II—with an average enrollment of 563 students in 2005–2006.

Funding flows from the Education Institute[11] directly to Independent schools and comprises three broad categories of support—*start-up funds* designed to cover preoperational expenses, *per-pupil allotments* based on enrollments, and *grants* to fund special projects or cover unusual needs. In addition, schools can earn small amounts of *miscellaneous income* on their own.

---

[10] "Model schools were developed in the 1970s to ease the transition from home to school for young boys, as well as to provide more employment opportunities for female teachers. A model school is a boys' primary school of four grades (1–4) in which both the teaching staff and the administration are female" (Brewer et al., 2007, p. 23).

[11] The Finance Office collects various types of financial information. Our analyses used the following sources of data, provided to us by the Finance Office:

- audited statements for 2004–2005 and 2005–2006
- cash flow statements for 2004–2005 and 2005–2006
- staffing reports for 2004–2005, 2005–2006, and 2006–2007
- finance office data on student enrollment for 2004–2005 and 2005–2006 on.

These data sources are described in detail in Appendix A, including all assumptions that we made to render these data comparable over time.

### Start-Up Funds

These funds were offered only to schools that were in the first year of operation and covered expenses from the day the contract was signed to the day the school opened for the beginning of the academic year. Start-up funds have typically covered such expenditures as administrative staff and teachers' stipends, professional development and training, recruitment of teachers and students, consultation fees, and library development. Start-up funds do not cover capital expenditures or procurements provided directly by the Education Institute, such as laboratories, furniture, and computers. In 2004–2005, the amount of start-up funds differed, depending on the amounts requested by each school. In 2005–2006, however, the Education Institute capped the amount at QR 500,000.[12] As of the 2006–2007 school year, the Education Institute halted the practice of offering start-up funds altogether. Instead, start-up funds are now provided as an advance on the per-pupil allotment (described below) given to schools, rather than as a separate source of revenue for the school.

### Per-Pupil Allotments

Schools receive per-pupil funding, disbursed quarterly, designed to cover operational expenses based on enrollment levels. The amount given to schools depends on the school's level (primary, preparatory, or secondary), with students with special needs qualifying for 20 percent augmentation of the per-pupil allotment. In 2005–2006, per-pupil allotments were QR 16,000 for primary, QR 19,400 for preparatory, and QR 21,800 for secondary schools from 2004 through 2006 (Education Institute, 2004, p. 8). The complexes received a mixture of per-pupil allotments based upon the number of students enrolled at each level.

### Grants

In 2004–2005, schools were offered the opportunity to apply for grants to cover any "non-operational expense necessary to encourage creativ-

[12] We found that schools were sometimes provided more and sometimes less than this amount of start-up funds in that year, however.

ity and innovation" in designing a school (Education Institute, 2004, p. 15). Grants typically covered major projects, such as special technological equipment, computer software, language programs, text books, special needs, and other activities not included in the operational budget. Grants were more or less discontinued in 2005–2006, however, and not offered in subsequent school years.

### Miscellaneous Income

This represents other income schools might earn, such as special tuition, cafeteria income, and the sale of books.

Figure 2.3 shows the breakdown of total funding into its component parts. As can be seen in the figure, the vast majority of funding consists of per-pupil allotments, ranging from 87 to 95 percent of the total funding, depending on the generation and year. For Generation I schools in their first year of operations, other funding

**Figure 2.3**
**Breakdown of Total Funding for Generation I and Generation II Independent Schools from September 1, 2004, Through August 31, 2005, and from September 1, 2005, Through June 30, 2006**

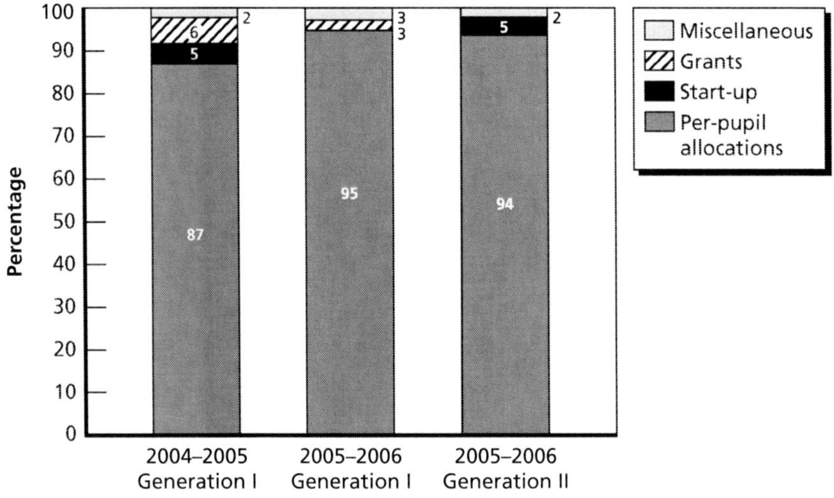


SOURCE: Finance Office: KPMG audited statements.
NOTE: Percentages may not sum to 100 percent because of rounding.
RAND *MG839-2.3*

consisted of grants (6 percent), start-up funds (5 percent), and miscellaneous income (2 percent). Per-pupil allocations accounted for a much larger share of total funding for Generation I schools in 2005–2006 than in the previous year (94 percent, compared with 87 percent), as start-up funding disappeared as a source of income and the total amount of grants was cut roughly in half (from 6 to 3 percent).[13] Generation II schools received 94 percent of their total funding in the form of per-pupil allocations. Almost no grants were awarded (only two out of 21 Generation II schools received any grants), and about 5 percent came from start-up funds.

## Independent School Revenues on a Per-Pupil Basis

Given that revenues are primarily driven by enrollment, comparing them on a per-pupil basis provides a meaningful way to measure funding differences across generations and operational years. We make two comparisons. The first (across generations) is between the first year of operation of Generation I schools (2004–2005) and the first year of operation of Generation II schools (2005–2006). The second (across operational years) is between the first year of operation for Generation I schools (2004–2005) and the second year of operation for these same schools (2005–2006).

Differences across school cohorts or across time may be driven by four primary factors. First, *policy changes* may affect school finances. For example, changing the status of Independent schools from for-profit to nonprofit and restricting operator compensation and surpluses might have provided incentives for schools to spend more. On the other hand, the provision of start-up funding in the first year of operations but not in subsequent years likely reduced per-pupil funding in subsequent years. And the cap on start-up funds and discontinuation of grants may have meant that Generation II schools received less funding

[13] Note that the vast majority of Generation I grants (97 percent) for the second year of operations were for a vocational school with a technology-intensive model that received a large grant. The remainder (3 percent) went to one other school and the remaining ten Generation I schools did not receive any grants in 2005–2006.

than did Generation I schools in their respective first years of operations. Second, schools and operators in the first and second generations may have been *selected* differently. For example, the SEC started converting large schools and the complexes first as part of its conversion plan. Schools in Generations I, II, and subsequent generations may use resources differently, have a different size and structure, and have students with different levels of performance and expectations. Conceivably, the operations of larger schools (e.g., economies of scale) or newer schools (e.g., differences in organizational and teaching practices) may differ from those of smaller or older schools. Third, as more and more Independent schools come online, the *scale* of the reform increases. The system is still very much in flux, which may also affect the comparison. Fourth, schools may have improved their operations after a year of experience in managing their finances. One might expect financial operations to be adjusted as a result of *learning* how to operate in the new environment. Conceptually, these two comparisons (across time and across cohort) and the factors driving change are shown in Figure 2.4. We illustrate and compare our findings, broken out across these dimensions, throughout the next section.

Figures 2.5 and 2.6 display the per-pupil revenue comparisons. Figure 2.5 shows the average per-pupil allocations[14] and other sources of revenue (start-up funds, grants, and miscellaneous income) on a per-pupil basis for Generation I schools for 2004–2005 and for 2005–2006 and for Generation II schools for 2005–2006. In a similar fashion, Figure 2.6 shows a detailed breakout of the three components (start-up funds, grants, and miscellaneous income) of other revenues.

Figure 2.5 shows that Generation I Independent schools received, on average, QR 19,868 per pupil in total funding in 2004–2005 and QR 18,320 in 2005–2006.[15] Generation II Independent schools received,

---

[14] Differences between our estimates of per-pupil allocations and expected allocations are likely the result of small numbers of students registering and withdrawing from the school within the year.

[15] One secondary school with a vocational curriculum, accounts for a significant portion of other sources of revenue as a result of a large grant. Without that school, other sources of revenues per pupil would be QR 2,225 and QR 473 per pupil in 2004–2005 and 2005–2006, respectively.

**Figure 2.4**
**Conceptual Representation of the Changes in Conditions Between Generation and Operational Year for Independent Schools**

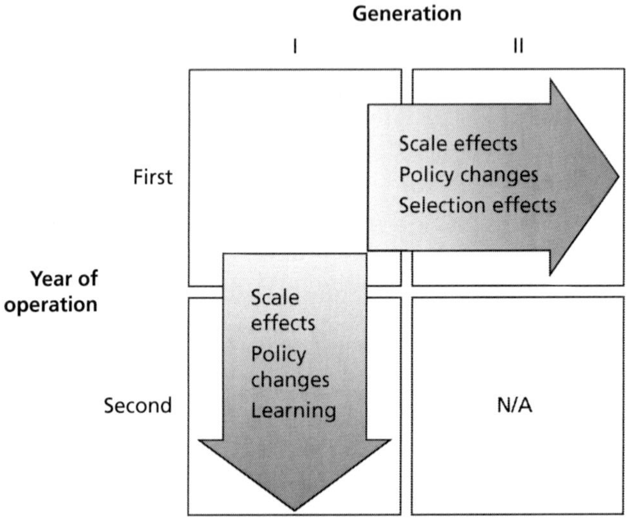


RAND *MG839-2.4*

on average, QR 19,011 per-pupil in total funding for the 2005–2006 operational year. Other revenues decreased from 13 percent of total revenues in the first year of operation to only 5 percent in the second year for Generation I schools.[16] Other revenues represented 6 percent of the total in the first year of operations of the Generation II schools.

Average per-pupil allocations varied primarily as a result of differences in school level, as shown in Table 2.2. Schools' per-pupil allocations, set by Finance Office policy, are estimated at about QR 16,000 for primary, QR 19,400 for preparatory, and QR 21,800 for secondary schools.[17] Finally, the two large complexes have a mixture of student

---

[16] Other revenues would change to 11 and 3 percent of total revenues, respectively, when we exclude from the analysis the secondary vocational school that accounts for a significant portion of other sources of revenue that resulted from a large grant.

[17] Differences between our estimates of per-pupil allocations and expected allocations are likely the result of small numbers of students registering and withdrawing from the school within the year.

**Figure 2.5**
**Per-Pupil Resource Allocations and Other Sources of Revenue for Generation I and Generation II Independent Schools, 2004–2005 and 2005–2006**

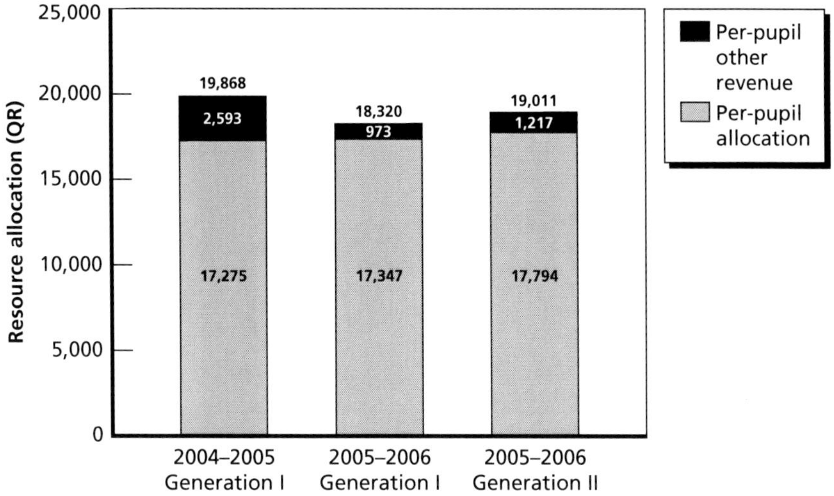


SOURCE: Finance Office: KPMG audited statements.
RAND *MG839-2.5*

levels and, hence, their average per-pupil allotments fell between the primary and preparatory school levels.

Figure 2.6 breaks out the category of other revenues. Comparing the first year of operations of Generation I schools with the first year of operations of Generation II schools, we see that Generation I schools were treated more generously, receiving QR 950 per pupil in start-up funding and QR 1,150 per pupil in grants, compared with QR 850 per pupil in start-up funding and virtually zero in grants.[18] Excluding miscellaneous income, which is not provided by the SEC, the additional support (on top of the basic per-pupil allocation funding) that

---

18 Excluding one secondary school with a vocational curriculum, which received a large grant, we find that Generation I schools received QR 964 per pupil in start-up funding and QR 814 per pupil in grants, compared with QR 850 per pupil in start-up funding and virtually zero in grants for Generation II schools.

**Figure 2.6**
**Per-Pupil Start-Up Funds, Grants, and Miscellaneous Income for Generation I and Generation II Independent Schools, 2004–2005 and 2005–2006**

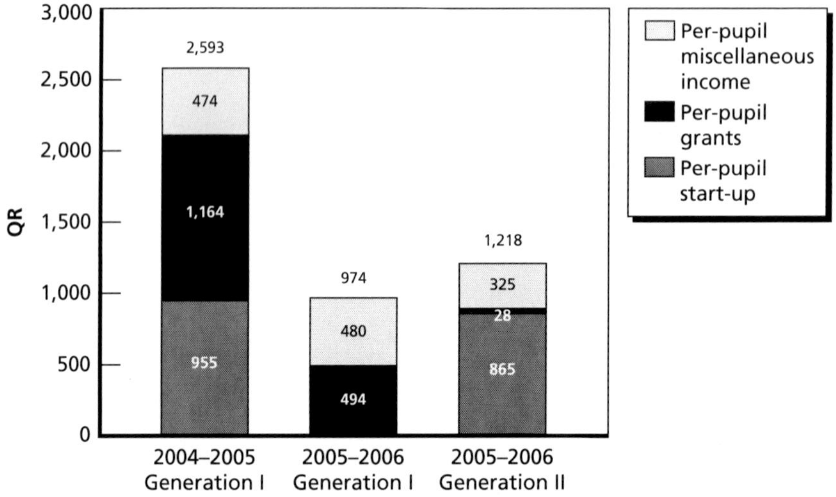


SOURCE: Finance Office: KPMG audited statements.
RAND *MG839-2.6*

**Table 2.2**
**Estimated Per-Pupil Allocations to Independent Schools, by Generation, Level, and School Year**

| School Type | Min | Max | Average | No. |
|---|---|---|---|---|
| Primary Generation I, 2004–2005 | 15,650 | 17,008 | 16,065 | 7 |
| Primary Generation I, 2005–2006 | 15,756 | 16,043 | 15,958 | 7 |
| Preparatory Generation I, 2004–2005 | 18,273 | 19,656 | 18,964 | 2 |
| Preparatory Generation I, 2005–2006 | 19,170 | 19,420 | 19,295 | 2 |
| Secondary Generation I, 2004–2005 | 21,400 | 21,400 | 21,400 | 1 |
| Secondary Generation I, 2005–2006 | 21,346 | 21,346 | 21,346 | 1 |
| Complexes Generation I, 2004–2005 | 17,870 | 18,082 | 17,976 | 2 |
| Complexes Generation I, 2005–2006 | 17,940 | 18,029 | 17,984 | 2 |
| Primary Generation II, 2005–2006 | 13,941 | 16,026 | 15,695 | 11 |
| Preparatory Generation II, 2005–2006 | 19,195 | 19,476 | 19,304 | 6 |
| Secondary Generation II, 2005–2006 | 21,061 | 21,641 | 21,409 | 4 |

SOURCES: Finance Office; KPMG audited statements.

Generation I schools received in their first year of operations was nearly 2.3 times greater than that received by Generation II schools on a per-pupil basis. This was due to both policy changes, consisting of a reduction in grant monies issued, and to selection effects, in that certain Generation I schools with specialized curricula obtained large grants to support their programs. Note that other sources of revenue account for only about 5–10 percent of total revenue—i.e., the overall differences in funding are still relatively small.

Although Generation I schools received more support in start-up funding than Generation II schools did in their first year of operation because of the enforcement of the QR 500,000 cap per school in 2005–2006, the amount of start-up funding per pupil is comparable. The apparent difference disappears on a per-pupil basis as a result of the larger average school sizes of Generation I schools, including, for example, two large complexes.

In the second year of Generation I school operations, no grants were provided except for one grant of QR 4.9 million and a relatively small grant of QR 133,000. The Generation II schools typically did not receive funding through grants, with the exception of a grant of QR 126,000 and one of QR 204,000. Thus, Generation II schools received less additional funding (on top of per-pupil allocations) in their first year of operations than Generation I schools did in their first year of operations.

Figure 2.7 shows that, on average, Independent schools carried surpluses in both 2004–2005 and 2005–2006. Surpluses as a percentage of operating revenues were, on average, 15 percent for Generation I schools in the first year of operation and 10 percent in the second year. Generation II schools had surpluses comparable with Generation I (16 percent) in their first year of operation, despite less access to start-up and grant support funding. It appears from these data that Independent schools were more hesitant to spend in their first year of operations but adjusted in their second year, suggesting that some organizational "learning" had occurred. Surpluses differed widely across

**Figure 2.7**
**Per-Pupil Operating Revenues, Expenditures, and Surpluses for Generation I and Generation II Schools, 2004–2005 and 2005–2006**

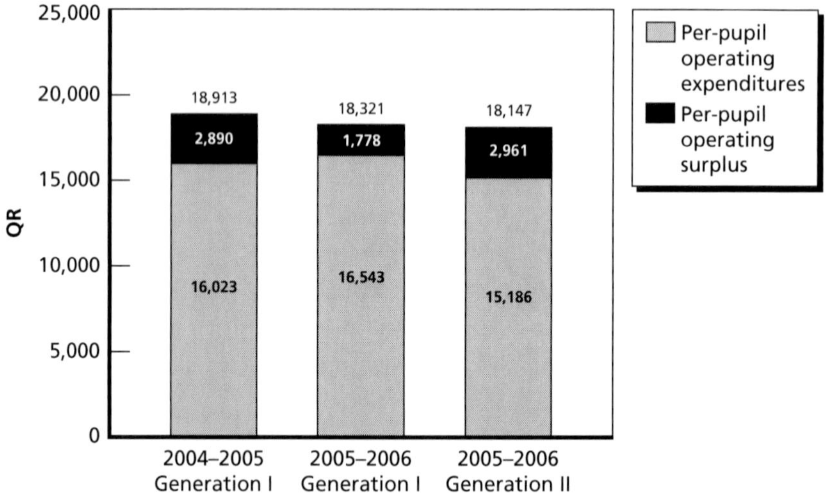


SOURCE: Finance Office: KPMG audited statements.
RAND *MG839-2.7*

schools, however—from –0.4 percent to 29 percent—although only one school in one year carried a deficit.[19]

We can speculate on several possible reasons for the accumulation of surpluses. First, a climate of uncertainty surrounding fiscal policies may have led operators to maintain high balances for contingency funds. This sense of instability may have been one reason schools were hesitant to spend. Second, new Independent schools may have lacked the time or expertise to address spending decisions and make purchases in a timely manner—a lack of readiness that might disappear over time as the schools settle into routine operation. Interviews with Education

[19] The –0.4 percent deficit was the only deficit and was for a Generation I secondary boys' school with a technology-intensive curriculum in its first year of operation. This school had a much higher cost base, which was funded by special grants. Although this school is significantly different from other Independent schools, excluding it from the sample does not change the conclusion that surpluses as a percentage of operating revenues differed widely by school. The new range in surpluses would be from 3 percent to 28 percent.

Institute officials indicated that they perceived operators as lacking in experience and encouraged operators to be less hesitant in spending the school's budget. Third, the system provided an incentive for operators to produce surpluses, as Independent schools were originally set up as for-profit entities.[20] Fourth, the system lacked direct incentives to increase quality, since accountability mechanisms were not tied to academic performance. Fifth, the requirement that all expenses were to be approved by the Finance Office may have led to underspending. Last, schools may simply have been overfunded and not have needed the amount of money they were given.

## Staff Expenditures

Among operating expenditure categories, staffing expenditures (defined generally in the audited statements as salaries and wages, retirement and health benefits, end of service benefits, bonuses, and rewards) represented the largest share. The percentage of total expenditures devoted to staffing was 80 and 81 percent, for the first and second year of operation of Generation I, respectively, and 84 percent for Generation II. Figure 2.8 displays trends in the numbers of teachers and nonteachers.[21] The teacher category is the largest staff group at Independent schools. With the increase from 12 Independent schools in 2004–2005 to 46 in 2006–2007, the total number of staff more than tripled over the three-year period. The nonteacher group grew at a faster rate (300 percent) than the teacher group (200 percent). The figure also shows the ratio of teachers to pupils. The ratio is relatively flat, suggesting that most of the increase in the number of teachers is due to the expansion of the reform.

---

[20] The original legal status of Independent schools and the subsequent transformation from for-profit to nonprofit entities is described in detail in Chapter Three.

[21] Individuals classified as teacher aides (69 in 2004, two in 2005, and three in 2006) are grouped in the nonteacher category.

**Figure 2.8**
**Number of Teaching and Nonteaching Staff in Independent Schools, Actual and Per Pupil, 2004–2007**

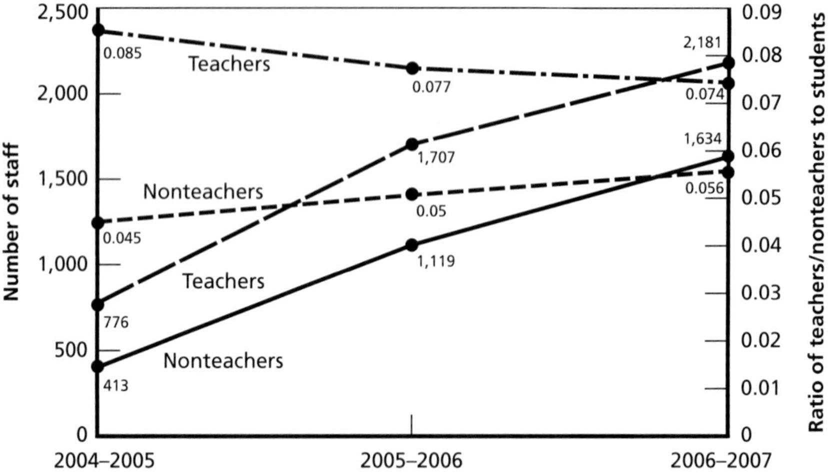


SOURCE: Office of Finance Staffing Reports.
RAND *MG839-2.8*

Table 2.3 estimates approximate numbers of staff in different job categories by gender.[22] In 2006–2007, females represented about 70

[22] The staffing reports from which we drew our data identified a large variety of nonstandard subject/title categories—more than 500 unique categories—and it was often difficult to tell from the names of the categories whether an individual was a teacher, a particular type of administrator, or another type of employee. Thus, our classifications may be subject to error. After isolating text strings such as "teacher," "Teacher," "instructor," etc., to create our aggregate job title categories, we scanned all job titles within categories to be sure that we had classified individuals into the category that best appeared to describe their jobs. Assignments that were not clear had job titles that were either abbreviated or did not fit into one of the main categories. Job titles in later years were more precise and, thus, 2004–2005 had a higher share of job titles that could not be placed into a main category. In 2004–2005, 19 percent of the job titles did not fall into the main title categories and were classified as "other," and less than 1 percent of cases were missing a job title. In 2005–2006, 7 percent of the job titles did not fall into the main title categories and were classified as "other," and about 4 percent of cases were missing a job title. And in 2006–2007, 6 percent of the job titles did not fall into the main title categories and were classified as "other," and about 3 percent of cases were missing a job title.

**Table 2.3**
**Distribution of Independent School Employees, by Job Category, Gender, and School Year**

| | 2004–2005 | | 2005–2006 | | 2006–2007 | |
|---|---|---|---|---|---|---|
| | No. | Percent | No. | Percent | No. | Percent |
| Male teachers | 212 | 18.3 | 431 | 15.3 | 681 | 17.9 |
| Female teachers | 564 | 48.7 | 1,276 | 45.2 | 1,500 | 39.3 |
| Male nonteachers | 91 | 7.9 | 290 | 10.3 | 462 | 12.1 |
| Female nonteachers | 292 | 25.2 | 829 | 29.3 | 1,171 | 30.7 |
| Total | 1,159 | 100 | 2,826 | 100 | 3,814 | 100 |

SOURCE: Office of Finance Staffing Reports.
NOTE: In 2004–2005, 30 noninstructional staff records did not contain gender information, and in 2006–2007, one noninstructional staff record did not contain gender information.

percent of all staff and 68 percent of all teachers in Independent schools. Female teachers constituted 50 percent of all employees in Independent schools, followed by female nonteachers (25 percent), male teachers (18 percent), and male nonteachers (8 percent).

Figure 2.9 illustrates trends in compensation using reported monthly total salaries. Our analysis of compensation is limited to the 2004–2005 and 2005–2006 years because salary data for 2006–2007 were incomplete.[23] We see that the average salaries of both teachers and nonteachers grew by about 6 percent (from QR 7,788 to QR 8,291 per month) for teachers and about 8 percent (QR 7,455 to QR 8,061) for nonteachers between 2004–2005 and 2005–2006.

Table 2.4 provides information on the monthly salaries (typically paid over 12 months) of teachers and of categories of staff involved in management of the schools. Again, these categorizations are

[23] The majority of 2006–2007 Staffing Reports use a "paid salary" category rather than a "total salary" category, whereas earlier reports used the latter category exclusively. The former category represents total salary after deductions for pensions, absences, and other items, whereas the latter category represents overall monthly salary as specified in the contract for each individual. Therefore salaries reported in the 2006–2007 reports are not comparable to those reported earlier.

**Figure 2.9**
**Average Monthly Teacher and Nonteacher Salaries in Independent Schools, 2004–2005 and 2005–2006**

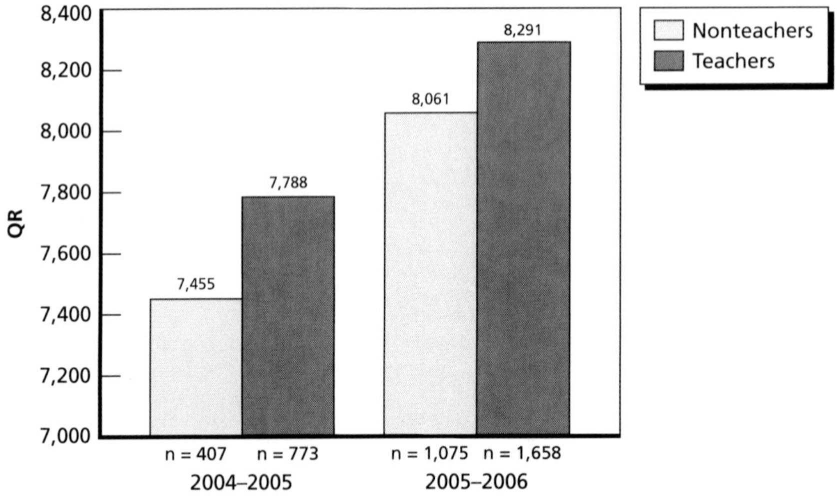


SOURCE: Office of Finance Staffing Reports: staff salaries.
NOTES: In 2004, six nonteacher and three teacher staff records were missing salary data. In 2005, 44 nonteacher and 49 teacher staff records were missing salary data.
RAND *MG839-2.9*

**Table 2.4**
**Average Monthly Total Salaries, by Select Job Categories (in QR)**

| | 2004–2005 | | | | | 2005–2006 | | | | |
|---|---|---|---|---|---|---|---|---|---|---|
| **Job Title** | **No.** | **Mean** | **Std. Dev.** | **Min** | **Max** | **No.** | **Mean** | **Std. Dev.** | **Min** | **Max** |
| Operator or principal | 16 | 24,294 | 5,370 | 15,000 | 30,000 | 48 | 20,906 | 5,782 | 10,000 | 37,040 |
| Vice principal | 23 | 15,906 | 3,991 | 8,500 | 23,000 | 34 | 16,299 | 4,686 | 6,000 | 27,230 |
| Subject head | 37 | 9,803 | 3,358 | 3,000 | 15,360 | 77 | 9,923 | 3,738 | 1,050 | 20,000 |
| Teacher | 773 | 7,788 | 2,535 | 1,230 | 16,500 | 1,658 | 8,291 | 2,472 | 2,500 | 23,000 |
| Total | 849 | | | | | 1,817 | | | | |

SOURCE: Office of Finance Staffing Reports.

approximate and are based on matching words in the subject/title field with the aggregate category that seemed most appropriate.

The leaders of Independent schools consisted of operators and principals. In 2004–2005, because Independent schools had initially been set up as for-profit Limited Liability Corporations (LLCs) formed by two or more partners, there were typically two operators per school and one principal, although some operators also functioned as principals. Operators could receive a salary, but they expected to receive at least a portion of their compensation in the form of profits. The designations of operator, operator-principal, and principal were inconsistent, sometimes overlapping, and difficult to compare over time. We therefore combined the categories together into one: operator or principal. Their average salary was less in 2005–2006 than in 2004–2005. This appears to be the result of fewer high-paid operators in the upper end of the salary range in later years as the Education Institute, following SEC directives, began to restrict operator earnings. Vice principals earned slightly less than operators/principals, and although each Independent school may have had its own administrative structure, one vice principal typically oversaw administrative affairs, whereas the other oversaw academic affairs. Subject heads earned more than regular teachers in Independent schools. They reported directly to the operator/principal or vice principal on matters related to curriculum and academic planning in the subject in which they specialized and also often conducted or coordinated professional development programs for teachers. For all job categories examined, we found a considerable range of variation.

## Summary

We estimated trends in expenditures and funding in the Qatar K–12 education reform between 2003–2004 and 2005–2006 as well as resource allocation within Independent schools. Our primary findings can be summarized as follows:

- Total expenditures on the reform grew from QR 144 million in 2003–2004 to QR 526 million in 2004–2005 and 841 million in 2005–2006.
- Independent school operating expenditures made up 37 and 48 percent of the total expenditures on the reform in 2004–2005 and 2005–2006, respectively.
- For Generation I Independent schools, revenues declined while expenditures increased in the second year of operation. Start-up funding disappeared and the total amount of grants was roughly cut in half.
- Comparing per-pupil funding for Generation I and Generation II schools in their first year of operation, we find that the former were treated more generously, receiving QR 950 per pupil in start-up funding and QR 1,150 per pupil in grants, compared with QR 850 per pupil in start-up funding and virtually zero in grants for Generation II schools.
- Independent schools appeared hesitant to spend in their first year of operations but adjusted their spending upward to some degree in their second year
  - Nearly all Independent schools carried surpluses as a percentage of operating revenues.
  - Average surpluses decreased for Generation I schools in their second year. Surpluses were, on average, 15 percent for Generation I schools in the first year of operation and 10 percent in the second year.
  - Generation II schools had surpluses comparable with Generation I surpluses (16 percent) in their first year of operation despite lower funding levels.
- Staff expenditures made up the majority of the operational expenditures of Independent schools (about 82 percent), with instructional staff accounting for approximately three-quarters of all staff expenditures. Rough estimates of the average salaries of teachers show that they grew by 6 percent between 2004–2005 and 2005–2006. Average salaries of nonteachers grew by 8 percent over the same period.

CHAPTER THREE

# Evaluation of the Reform's School Finance System

The descriptive analyses provided in Chapter Two summarize expenditure and funding patterns in the reform throughout its first three years. We now turn to the key question of whether the reform's school finance system is meeting the objectives of a sound system. We evaluate the system on the basis of its adherence to a set of guiding principles. A review of the literature on school finance yielded several characteristics that appeared to be related to a highly functioning school finance system.[1] We synthesized these into the following six guiding principles:

1. *Transparency*: A school finance system should be based on a clear accounting system that tracks the use of funds.
2. *Equity*: A school finance system should provide resources sufficient to meet the needs of all students equitably.
3. *Adequacy*: A school finance system should provide funding that is adequate to support educational excellence.
4. *Efficiency*: A school finance system will deliver effective educational models at the most economical price.
5. *Accountability*: A school finance system should ensure that recipients of public funds produce a quality of education commensurate with the funding received.
6. *Stability/responsiveness*: A school finance system will balance the stability in funding needed to enable schools to invest in the

[1] See, for example, Cheng (1993), Hanushek and Luque (2003), Hanushek (2003), Marzano (2000), and Scheerens and Bosker (1997).

high-quality delivery of education with the flexibility to adjust to ongoing evidence-based needs assessments.

We evaluate the system against each of these objectives in turn. The evaluation points to recommendations to improve the school system's performance as it evolves.

## Transparency

To achieve transparency, a school finance system needs a data system that is comprehensive, accurate, and comparable across institutions and time periods. In addition, data must be easily accessed by institutional researchers and in sufficient detail to support the types of analyses that inform policymaking.

The Office of Shared Services and the Finance Office collect a rich variety of data, which are vital to tracking the progress of the reform. However, several data-related issues made it difficult to produce accurate and complete analyses for the period covered by this monograph, and it is useful to outline the primary obstacles to analysis. Some of these issues may have since been resolved with the introduction of a new management information system. As of fall 2008, this new system had been partially implemented in Independent schools.

First, the time periods covered by various financial documents were not standardized. Thus, data could not be compared across time periods. For example, the Office of Shared Services reported financial information for the fiscal year (April 1 through March 31) on some documents and for the periods from April 1 through July 15 and from July 16 through March 31 on others. Although the data allowed some corrections to be made to obtain financial information for each fiscal year at the aggregate level, such corrections were not possible for much of the more detailed information (such as the breakdown of institute spending or of assets procurement), as the categories for expenses had changed between the 2004–2005 and 2005–2006 reporting. As a result, we could compare total expenditures on the reform between fiscal years only at the aggregate level but not in detail.

In addition, the Finance Office provided audited statements prepared by auditing firms KPMG and Deloitte & Touche regarding the operation of each Independent school for the academic year (September 1 through August 31), which could therefore not be compared with shared services data reported for the fiscal year. Furthermore, monthly cash flow statements were not available for every school over the same time period. As a result, cash flow data could not be used to analyze the financial operations of Independent schools. We examined only the ratio of total administrative to total instructional wages, judging that although actual total wages might change over time, the ratio was likely to be fairly stable. However, all other cash flow data, such as allocations across spending on supplies, professional development, maintenance, etc., could not be used in comparisons.

Second, financial categorizations were not reported in a standard format. We found that many individual schools did not use the standard categories prescribed in the financial handbook (Education Institute, 2004) when reporting their cash flow statements, and that data were not available for each school for the same time period. This could result either because schools did not perceive a need to report using the standard categories or they felt that the standard categories did not meet their reporting needs. The school personnel reports—called the Staffing Reports—were particularly inconsistent across schools. Job titles were inconsistently defined, and data were incomplete. Reporting dates differed by school. The salary measure was not reported in a consistent manner across time, so we could not compare salaries in 2006–2007 with salaries in earlier years. Staff identification numbers did not appear to be consistently maintained across time. These problems rendered analyses of salary trends by job category subject to a large margin of error. In some cases, important analyses were not possible, such as analyses to determine attrition rates. Tracking teacher attrition is important to policymakers in structuring pay scales and other incentives, such as bonuses or improvements in working conditions.

Third, the level of detail in the data was sometimes insufficient. In particular, the Staffing Reports failed to provide complete information on unique identifiers; characteristics of staff, such as the job title, level of education, and years of experience; and different components of salary (total salary, different types of benefits, and paid salary). For example, separating the subject taught from the job title would help determine whether shortages of particular categories of personnel, say science teachers, exist or whether salaries differ by subject. The Staffing Reports lacked information on basic job categories, and it was often difficult to determine the type of work an individual performed. Information on standardized job categories would have made the analyses more reliable. A recommended set of categories to be implemented going forward might include the following:

- principal/operator
- vice principal
- professional administrative (e.g., guidance counselors, business managers, nurses, librarians, information technology personnel)
- nonprofessional administrative (e.g., clerical)
- subject head
- teacher
- teacher aide or assistant
- other instructional staff (e.g., special education resource specialists, sports coaches)
- facilities staff (e.g., janitorial staff, guards, bus drivers, cafeteria workers).

To be available for research and truly inform policymaking, data need to be accessible for analytic and monitoring purposes to policymakers and decisionmakers, institutional researchers, analysts, educators, and families (with levels of access differing among these stakeholder groups). In many cases, schools sent hard copies of data, rather than electronic copies, to the Finance Office, necessitating manual input before analyses could be performed. Thus, although such data were accessible, there were significant barriers to their use.

## Equity

Equity concerns arise when disadvantaged groups are shortchanged in the allocation of resources within a system. Equity is therefore assessed by examining differences in resource allocation across different groups of students. In the Qatar public school system, disadvantaged groups have not officially been identified by the government, so we do not discuss them here. However, given that clear differences exist in the staff characteristics of girls' and boys' schools, we analyzed school finances by gender to provide information regarding the financial balance between the two types of schools. Gender segregation may have an effect on school finances, given that wages account for the majority of school expenditures and female teachers earn less than their male counterparts.

Since female teachers can teach boys only through the primary school level, and since primary, preparatory, and secondary schools received different amounts of funding, we investigated gender breakdowns by school level. The analysis of gender by level focused only on the 21 Generation II schools in 2005–2006, because there were insufficient numbers of schools in certain levels of Generation I in some categories[2] and because the Generation I complexes do not provide financial breakdowns by level.

Inspection of 2005–2006 finance data indicates that average per-pupil allocations and other sources of revenues (start-up funding, grants, and miscellaneous income) show only slight differences for boys' and girls' schools at each level (see Figure 3.1).[3] The slight difference in other revenues for boys' and girls' schools is due to start-up funds, grants,

---

[2] In Generation I, there are only two boys' schools and no girls' schools at the preparatory level. There is only one secondary boys' school, and there are no girls' schools at the secondary level. There is one boys' complex and one girls' complex.

[3] Per-pupil allocations are slightly below expected. Official per-pupil funding (Education Institute, 2004) is QR 16,000 for elementary schools, QR 19,400 for preparatory schools, and QR 21,800 for secondary schools, although Figure 3.2 shows QR 15,700 for elementary schools, QR 19,300 for preparatory schools, and QR 21,400 for secondary schools. Differences are likely the result of small numbers of students registering and withdrawing from the school within the year.

**Figure 3.1**
**Per-Pupil Revenue Allocations and Other Sources of Revenue for Generation II Independent Schools on a Per-Pupil Basis from September 1, 2005, Through June 30, 2006, by School Level and School Gender**

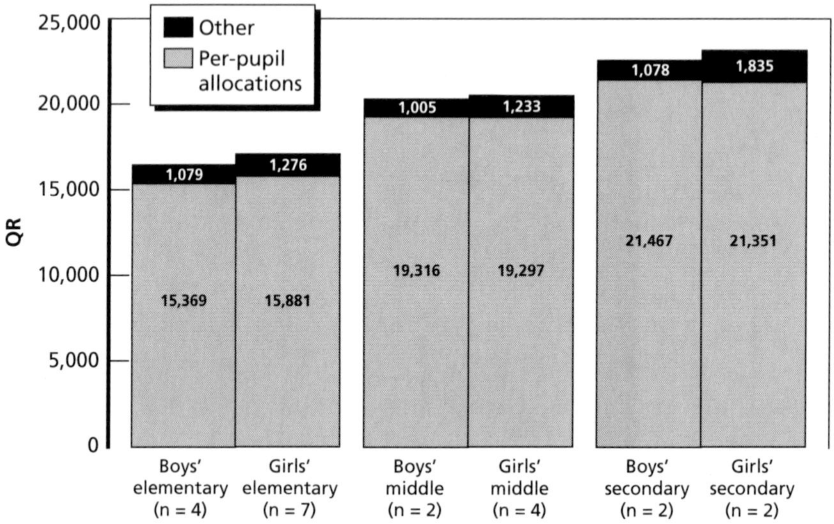


SOURCE: Finance Office: KPMG audited statements.
RAND *MG839-3.1*

and miscellaneous funds. Boys' schools received slightly less start-up funds (QR 471,658, on average, compared with QA 499,353 for girls' schools) and these were spread across larger numbers of pupils—boys' schools had an average of 583 pupils and girl's schools had an average of 551 students per school. Only two Generation II schools received grants in 2005–2006, and both were girls' preparatory schools.[4] In addition, one secondary girls' school generated miscellaneous income of QR 1,330 per pupil (compared with QR 420 per pupil, on average, for all schools).

Similarly, there appears to be little difference between boys' and girls' schools at each level when comparing operating revenues, expenditures, and surpluses (see Figure 3.2), except for an apparent

[4] KPMG financial statements indicated that one school received a grant to acquire property and equipment. Details on the use of the grant for the other school were not provided.

**Figure 3.2**
**Per-Pupil Operating Expenditures and Surpluses for Generation II Schools from September 1, 2005, Through June 30, 2006, by School Level and School Gender**

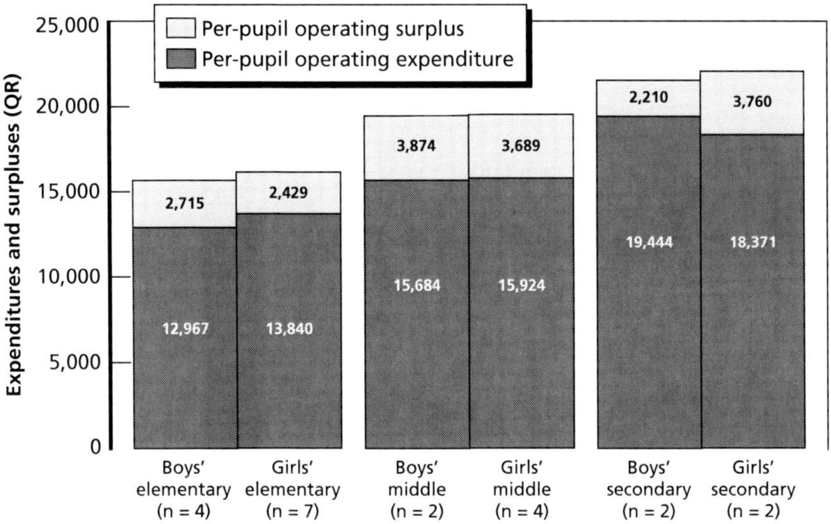


SOURCE: Finance Office: KPMG audited statements.
RAND *MG839-3.2*

difference in surpluses at the secondary school level in favor of girls' schools (one of the two girls' secondary schools had higher-than-average miscellaneous income per pupil). Overall, the data from this small sample of schools indicate that the finance system achieved a certain amount of gender parity, as very few differences exist in funding or expenditures by a school's gender.

However, the apparent similarities found in this sample of schools mask underlying differences in compensation. The financial balance is tenuous and depends on the offsetting effects of male/female and Qatari/non-Qatari salary differences. For example, changes in the salaries of Qataris relative to those of non-Qataris might shift the balance in staff spending between the boys' and girls' schools because girls' schools employ higher proportions of Qataris. For the same reason, changes in or stronger enforcement of the Qatarization quotas designed to increase the proportion of Qataris in the workforce might upset the balance in staff spending between boys' and girls' schools.

Figure 3.3 shows average monthly salary differences for teachers, by gender and nationality, in all Independent schools in 2004–2005 and 2005–2006. Qatari men are by far the highest-paid staff members in Independent schools. In 2004–2005, they earned around 52 percent more (QR 4,805), on average, than the next highest-earning category, Qatari women. This difference grew even more in 2005–2006, when Qatari men earned almost 60 percent more than Qatari women (a premium of QR 5,585).

Non-Qatari teachers of both genders received lower average salaries than Qatari teachers, although non-Qatari male teacher salaries were similar to those of Qatari female teachers in 2005–2006. Of particular interest in Figure 3.3 is the 20 percent increase over the two-year period in the average monthly salaries of non-Qatari male teachers, to the point where they are similar to the salaries of Qatari female

**Figure 3.3**
**Average Monthly Teacher Salaries in Independent Schools, by Teacher Gender and Nationality, 2004–2005 and 2005–2006**

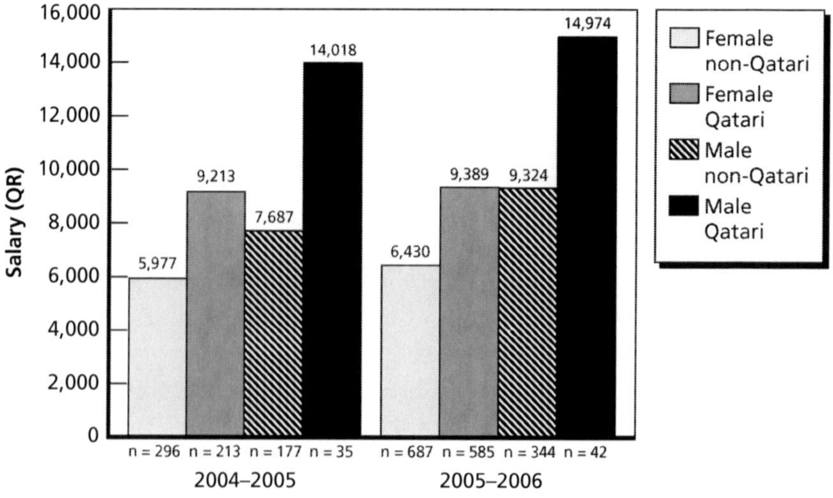


SOURCE: Office of Finance Staffing Reports: staff salaries.
RAND *MG839-3.3*

teachers. It is likely, then, that the observed parity in boys' and girls' schools' instructional expenses was an outcome of the salary parity between Qatari females and non-Qatari males. Although these results were based on a small sample of Independent schools, similar patterns are likely to operate in the full population of schools. The lowest earning category, female non-Qataris, earned substantially less, on average, than the other groups. In 2005–2006, individuals in this group earned, on average, between 45 and 46 percent less than those in the female Qatari and male non-Qatari categories, and they earned less than half of a male Qatari's average salary.

In sum, the apparent gender equity in school finance appears to be the result of a tenuous balance between teacher gender and nationality wage premiums and is based on unequal staff salaries for different gender and nationality groups. Proposed Qatarization policies may upset this balance, if enforced. If salary differentials remain in place while the staffing mix changes, the funding balance between boys' and girls' schools might be erased.

## Adequacy

Adequacy may be defined in terms of outcomes or inputs. There is no universally accepted definition of adequacy in education funding, and even when a definition is agreed on, there is debate over how to measure it (Augenblick, Myers, and Anderson, 1997; Picus, 2000; Guthrie and Springer, 2007). Several strategies have been developed to determine the funding levels adequate to achieve particular goals, but none has been accepted as definitive and each is subject to limitations. Nevertheless, at the end of the day, policymakers are left with the task of establishing funding levels for public school systems, despite the limitations of various approaches to doing so.

The convenience and growing availability of outcomes based on test scores has led to their popularity as a measure on which to base a determination of adequate funding. In the United States, many debates over whether a state provides enough funding for an adequate education have been decided in the courts, because state education systems have not been considered impartial (Picus, 2000). Recent court decisions in the United States have leaned toward defining adequacy in terms of a dollar amount of funding that is believed to be enough to achieve a desired level of student achievement on standardized tests.[5] Performance on standardized tests provides a valuable indicator of learning; however, it is important to keep in mind that it may fail to capture aspects of learning that are not measurable through these types of tests and it is only one of several possible measures, such as graduation rates and student or parent satisfaction, or delayed effects, such as college attendance or employment rates.

There are four main approaches to determining funding levels adequate to produce desired outcomes (Augenblick et al., 1997; Guthrie and Springer, 2007; and Hanushek, 2006). These are generally referred to as the historical approach, the professional judgment approach, the econometric approach, and the successful schools approach.

The *historical* approach merely assigns new funding levels based on past levels. It starts by setting a base-cost level using the actual expenditures of a given set of schools. Advantages include simplicity and predictability. A disadvantage appears if spending in previous years was not truly adequate or was too high. This method has no ability to distinguish between funding adequate to produce desired outcomes and funding adequate to produce past outcomes.

The *professional judgment* approach relies on a panel of experts to decide the resource levels needed to achieve a high-quality learning environment. Once the type and amount of resources are decided, they are assigned costs. The costs are then summed to produce a total spending amount. Although sensible, the professional judgment approach has some drawbacks. First, no clear selection criteria for the expert panel exist. Second, whether the panel is composed of educators or financial officers, conflicts of interest are likely. Third, the judgments made are likely to be highly subjective and lacking any connection to efficiency.

The *econometric* or "cost-function" approach examines the relationship between costs and education outcomes using econometric model-

---

[5] For example, the 2005 *West Orange Cove ISD v. Neeley* decision, in Texas, was based on analyses related to student achievement.

ing. Data on costs, achievement, and school characteristics (including the socioeconomic characteristics of their pupils) are collected. Costs are then related in a statistical model to achievement and school characteristics. Using the resulting statistical equation, predicted costs are calculated for a desired level of achievement.

The econometric approach is problematic for several reasons. First, the data are based on the existing use of resources, which may or may not be efficient. Second, and more important, the results are highly sensitive to the way the model is specified (Guthrie and Springer, 2007). Third, if desired achievement levels are much higher than those currently achieved in the sample of schools in the data, the equation must predict costs based on scanty evidence, which may lead to out-of-sample prediction bias. Last and most important, the model can be highly misleading if resources and achievement are only weakly related. If this relationship is not strong, then the model will produce very high and most likely inflated estimates of the amount of funding needed to produce small desired increases in student achievement (Hanushek, 2006).

The *successful schools* approach examines actual expenditures in schools that are viewed as successful in achieving desired outcomes, adjusting for factors that lead to bias, such as having students from high-income families. In this approach, high-performing schools are first identified, and average expenditures in these schools are then calculated and used as evidence of adequate spending levels.[6] One advantage of this method is that it can examine the use of several types of resources in high-performing schools and compare it with the use of these same resources in lower-performing schools. For example, per-pupil expenditures, pupil-teacher ratios, the ratio between administrative and instructional expenditures, etc., can all be examined. A dis-

---

[6] In the United States, John Augenblick and John Myers were the first to employ a successful schools methodology in response to the education adequacy order of the Ohio Supreme Court in *DeRolph v. State* (1997). They sought to identify school districts that were meeting state standards and then to use those districts' average expenditure amount as a fair estimate of the actual cost of an adequate education. After removing "outliers," the researchers chose a sample of successful school districts by reference to six specific measures of student achievement and eight input measures, such as pupil-teacher ratio and average teacher salary.

advantage is that it requires that the most successful schools do indeed reach desired performance levels—if they do not, there will be no truly successful schools from which to gather expenditure data.

After weighing the pros and cons of these various approaches, we deemed the successful schools approach—although subject to limitations as well—to be the most suitable methodology to apply to the Qatari context, because it relies on actual rather than hypothetical spending patterns and is not subject to the issues that undermine the credibility of the econometric approach. As a first step, we created school performance measures. The process of constructing such measures is complex and subject to a number of possible limitations. The simplest measure is average school performance. This measure is likely to be biased, however, by the nonrandom sorting of students into schools. In other words, if more-able students tend to select or be selected by particular schools, then the average performance measure will measure both the ability of the students and what the school itself has taught them, but it will be impossible to distinguish between the two components. Thus, it will be impossible to know whether the school—rather than its group of students—is truly "high-performing." To correct for this, some measure of a school's "value added" is generally constructed. This is done by adjusting in some fashion for the prior achievement of students and thus requires a minimum of two years of test scores for each student.

One way to create a rough measure of the value added by the school is to simply take the difference between a recent and a prior test score for each child and average these differences by school. A more fine-grained method of creating such a measure is to adjust for prior scores and, if possible, other student characteristics in a multivariate statistical regression model. By controlling for the students' prior year scores, we can better establish the net value added by the school in the current year and reduce the influence of performance based simply on the child's ability level relative to others at the beginning of the year. Adjusting for child characteristics further isolates the contribution to learning offered by the school. This is the method we used.

We constructed school performance measures by calculating school-level effects on 2005–2006 test scores after adjusting for

2004–2005 test performance and available child characteristics through a student-level multiple regression. The measures were constructed in separate regressions for each school level: primary, preparatory, and secondary. Since the complexes had students in each of these levels, their students appear in all three separate analyses.

The data on test scores come from the QCEA,[7] and the data for the covariates come from the parent survey responses in the QNEDS. The student characteristics accounted for in our statistical model include the student's gender, Qatari citizenship, age in months, grade level, mother's and father's education, parental involvement with the school and with homework, number of hours spent on homework, Arabic language primacy in the home, living in Doha, and having special needs.

After estimating this model,[8] we saved the adjusted school performance measures. We then compared the schools ranked in the top

---

7 The QCEA is a paper-and-pencil assessment battery that consists of multiple-choice and constructed-response questions, based on Qatar's curriculum standards in mathematics, science, Arabic, and English. For a more detailed description see Brewer et al. (2007).

8 The statistical model can be written as follows:

$$y_{ist} = \rho y_{it-1} + X_{ist}\beta + \alpha_{st} + \gamma LOSS_{ist} + \varepsilon_{ist}$$

where $y_{ist}$ is the achievement of child i in school s at time t, $y_{it-1}$ is the achievement of child i in the prior period t – 1 (independent of school s, as we allow for the possibility that a pupil changed schools), and X is the vector child-level characteristics listed above. The parameter $\rho$ represents the relationship between current and prior achievement. The vector of parameters $\beta$ represents the relationships between student achievement and each of the variables contained in X. The parameters $\alpha_{st}$ , which differ for each school, represent the deviation from average achievement for each school, after adjusting for all the other factors in the model. Thus, these estimates serve as our school performance measures. If a large and representative proportion of students switched schools from the prior year, a somewhat stronger model might be one that controlled for student fixed effects in estimating the school fixed effects, but given data limitations, this is not feasible except in the few grades that represent a transition, say from elementary to preparatory school. The present model was chosen in the interest of providing a uniform measure that could pool data across grades for a given school level.

In addition, we included an indicator for a student's having the lowest obtainable scale score (LOSS), because the tests contained strong floor effects largely because a number of children appeared not to have answered any questions, thus introducing measurement error. Inclusion of the LOSS indicator variable seemed the most parsimonious correction for the measurement problems.

half of the distribution of adjusted ranks to those ranked in the bottom half to see if there was a difference in per-pupil expenditures and pupil-teacher ratio. Table 3.1 shows these differences for the four types of tests and three types of levels.

From the table, we see that the primary schools scoring in the top half in Arabic, English, and mathematics spent more on these tests per pupil, on average, than those in the bottom half. The difference is statistically significant, even with the small number of schools in the analysis. There are some nonsignificant differences in spending at the preparatory and secondary levels, so these results provide little guidance in determining adequate resource use at these levels. Similar results are seen for the pupil-teacher ratios, where better test results for the Arabic and English exams in primary schools are associated with smaller class sizes. Again, the difference was statistically significant even with the small number of schools. It is worth noting that the average pupil-teacher ratio for schools in the top half is consistently better than the average parent-teacher ratio for schools in the bottom half for every test at every level but one (preparatory English), although the difference is not always statistically significant. The above analyses should be interpreted as merely suggestive, given the limited number of schools in the system. In addition, it is important to note that the school performance measures we have created are not exact measures of "true" school quality but instead are approximations. Our controls for student body characteristics may not adequately address possible selection bias resulting from differences in the particular types of students in different schools. Therefore, our results should be interpreted with caution.

However, our analysis suggests that spending slightly more than QR 15,000 per pupil in primary schools (at 2005–2006 prices) might produce relatively high performance levels in Arabic, English, and mathematics. Given that per-pupil revenue allocations at the primary school level are currently set at QR 16,000, they may be adequate to produce educational excellence, and it is possible that low-spending schools should be encouraged to spend more. However, this is a very preliminary observation based on fewer than 20 schools. Furthermore, determining a desired—or "excellent" level of adjusted school performance has yet to be established. This is outside the scope of our study

**Table 3.1**
**Resource Use in Independent Schools Ranked in the Top and Bottom Halves of the School Performance Distribution, 2005–2006**

| Test Type | School Type | No. of Schools | Per-Pupil Expenditure | Pupil-Teacher Ratio |
|---|---|---|---|---|
| Arabic | Top primary | 8 (2) | 14968.4[a] | 11.5[a] |
| | Bottom primary | 10 | 13555.6 | 14.1 |
| | Top preparatory | 4 (1) | 16087.5 | 13.3 |
| | Bottom preparatory | 4 (1) | 16373.4 | 14.2 |
| | Top secondary | 1 (2) | 18100.3 | 10.2 |
| | Bottom secondary | 3 | 25147.1[b] | 11.5 |
| English | Top primary | 8 (2) | 14856.0[a] | 11.7[a] |
| | Bottom primary | 10 | 13645.5 | 14.0 |
| | Top preparatory | 3 (2) | 16393.9 | 14.3 |
| | Bottom preparatory | 5 | 16132.4 | 13.4 |
| | Top secondary | 1 (2) | 18100.3 | 10.2 |
| | Bottom secondary | 3 | 25147.1[b] | 11.5 |
| Math | Top primary | 8 (2) | 14999.6[a] | 12.0 |
| | Bottom primary | 10 | 13530.6 | 13.8 |
| | Top preparatory | 3 (2) | 17253.2 | 13.7 |
| | Bottom preparatory | 5 | 15616.8 | 13.8 |
| | Top secondary | 1 (2) | 18100.3 | 10.2 |
| | Bottom secondary | 3 | 25147.1[b] | 11.5 |
| Science | Top primary | 8 (2) | 14174.6 | 13.0 |
| | Bottom primary | 10 | 14194.5 | 13.2 |
| | Top preparatory | 3 (2) | 16548.3 | 13.3 |
| | Bottom preparatory | 5 | 15700.6 | 14.6 |
| | Top secondary | 1 (2) | 18641.8 | 10.2 |
| | Bottom secondary | 3 | 24918.5[b] | 12.5 |

NOTES: The top/bottom rankings were created using the adjusted school performance measure including the two complexes. "No. of Schools" is the number of schools used in calculating the average per-pupil expenditure and does not include the two complexes, because their financial information was not broken out by level; the number of complexes is indicated in parentheses.

[a] Indicates a significant difference between the top and bottom halves at the 10 percent level.

[b] Note that the per-pupil expenditure numbers for secondary schools in the bottom half of the distribution include a vocational school with a technology-intensive curriculum, which has significantly higher per-pupil expenditure as a result of its curriculum focus. Excluding this school gives per-pupil expenditure values for these schools of QR 19,787 for the Arabic, English, and math test and QR 19,444 for the science test. Pupil-teacher ratio numbers change only slightly.

and would require the establishment of national proficiency targets based on these particular performance measures.[9]

To explore the relationship between resources and achievement further, we estimated the same regression model treating school effects as random and dependent on funding and pupil-teacher ratios. As our variables of interest were at the group (school) level, a school fixed-effects specification is not helpful. We find that both higher per-pupil expenditures and lower pupil-teacher ratios are significantly related to higher achievement on test scores. This result holds for nearly all of the exams (Arabic, English, math, and science), and across all school levels (primary, preparatory, and secondary). As an example, our estimates indicate that for an additional $100 spent per pupil per year on primary school education, one can expect to see an increase in Arabic test scores of one point. Because the average year-to-year increase in primary school is 17 points, an additional point represents a significant increase of more than 5 percent of the average annual increase on test scores. Similarly, an increase of one pupil per teacher is associated with a reduction in average test scores by one point.

The majority of top-performing schools are Generation I schools in their second year of operation (more than two-thirds of Generation I schools are top half performers in the three tests of statistical significance [Arabic, English, and math]). Since we found that schools tend to spend more of their budget in their second year, it may be that as they become more familiar with the new environment, development over time may contribute to the positive relationship between spending and performance.

The findings regarding adequate funding levels are not definitive. Rather, we have illustrated a methodology for determining school performance and tracking the spending levels of high-performing schools. This methodology will yield more conclusive findings as the number of schools grows, thus increasing the power of statistical analyses to detect significant relationships. The same methodology can be used to determine target levels for the use of other resources in schools as well

---

9 Student-level performance standards were developed by the Evaluation Institute in February 2006. However, school-level performance standards have not been established.

as overall per-pupil spending. For example, pupil-teacher ratios and the percentage of teachers with different characteristics (such as particular nationalities and education or experience levels) can be examined in the same manner once school performance measures have been constructed. In addition, multiple regression techniques can be used to determine the relationship of particular resources to school performance after adjusting for the use of other types of resources. It may be that some resources are more effective than others in improving learning. In the future, such analyses could serve as a guide in deciding where to shift resources within schools.

## Efficiency

An assessment of *efficiency* is based on a determination of the appropriate trade-off between school performance and the costs of producing it. This determination is difficult, because the number of schools that are performing at high levels is currently small. Therefore, we suggest methods to associate effectiveness with levels of spending to characterize relative operational efficiency in the schools.

We can think of economic efficiency as a ratio of benefits to costs. In theory, a school would be deemed most efficient by finding the point at which the added benefit of spending an extra unit of funding is smaller than the added cost. If adding more funding produces a marginally lower amount of gain, then it would not be efficient to spend more. However, efficiency is a difficult concept to operationalize. Often, efficiency is approached more heuristically by first establishing a desired target level of performance and then determining the minimum amount of funding that would produce this level. The first step is to determine school performance levels using methods that adjust for student characteristics in a way similar to that outlined in the previous section. The next step is to determine the level of school performance that is considered proficient. The third step is to select a set of schools that meet the standards for proficiency and examine their resource use. If enough schools can be identified as high-performing, it would be possible to compare expenditures across these schools and eliminate the high-spending schools from the calculation of average expenditures, because they are less efficient than high-performing, lower-spending schools. The resulting average expenditure estimate may then be considered efficient.

These comparisons are tied into the notion of productivity. Two otherwise equivalent schools might require different levels of funding to get the same test scores if one school is more productive than the other. The more-productive school achieves the same level of performance but at a lower cost. By examining school resource use in the manner suggested, better educational technologies can be identified and promulgated throughout the system.

With so few Independent schools at each level in our data, it is difficult to implement this methodology or draw conclusions regarding efficiency. With more subsequent conversions to Independent school status and with the establishment of national norms regarding adjusted standards for school performance, it will be possible to compare resource use across a larger number of high-performing schools and determine which schools are more efficient. It is also advisable to conduct case studies and possibly surveys of staff in high-performing schools to uncover the practices that make them successful. This approach can be particularly helpful in distinguishing schools that achieve high performance efficiently from those that do so inefficiently.

## Accountability

A key element of the Education for a New Era reform in Qatar is that Independent schools are held accountable to the community for fiscal responsibility and student learning. Thus far, accountability for the proper use of funds has been based primarily on these two mechanisms: fiscal monitoring and school choice. The first involves oversight by the Finance Office. The second involves parents' selecting the schools that their children attend—essentially "voting by one's feet" and signaling, to some degree, their satisfaction with the schools.

The Finance Office holds schools fiscally accountable through a monitoring process that tracks school expenditures and operator's resource allocation decisions. It does so through three methods: external audits, the set-up of an internal monitoring system at each school, and the creation of guidelines and requirements to which schools should or must adhere. External audits have been used since the beginning of the reform.[10] Second, schools must devise an internal monitoring system as part of their overall management strategy. This includes devising a set of policies and procedures regarding financial matters, a budget development calendar, a computer-based accounting system, a system for payroll services, and banking arrangements. Third, the Finance Office has developed a set of mandatory budget guidelines covering surpluses, financial operations, and salary floors for Qatari staff. Schools submit a number of reports throughout the year directly to the Finance Office so that it can assess compliance with these guidelines and work with schools to ensure that they are in compliance with the above reporting requirements.[11] The guidelines in effect in 2004–2005 and 2005–2006 were as follows:

1. Operators should allocate about 60 percent of the overall budget for instructional staff salaries and expenses.
2. Schools are encouraged to allocate not more than 17 percent of their budget to administration expenses.
3. Schools can move up to 10 percent of the budget amount from any line item to another. Any movement between line items beyond the above limits needs to be approved by the Finance Office.
4. Operators may not charge tuition for students entitled to government per-pupil funding.

---

[10] Auditing firms KPMG and Deloitte & Touche reported on the financial operations of the Generation I and II schools in 2004–2005 and 2005–2006.

[11] These reports include the following: before the school year starts (1) projected annual budget and (2) three-year budget projection; throughout the school year (1) September 1—annual projected cash flow and (2) quarterly—actual cash flow, staffing report, and enrollment report; each month, adjusted cash flow; beginning of June, projected operational budget for the next year; end of school year (1) independent fiscal audit report statement of functional expenses and (2) annual report.

We found that the majority of schools adhered to guidelines (1) and (2), with expenditures on instructional staff at 64 percent of the overall budget and expenditures on administrative staff expenditures at 19 percent of the overall budget on average, in the 2005–2006 school year.[12] We did not have information of sufficient detail to assess adherence to guidelines (3) and (4).

In addition to providing the above guidelines, the Finance Office has taken action with regard to budgetary surpluses and operator compensation. In 2004–2005, the Finance Office recommended that "During the initial years of opening, reinvestments into the schools is the preferred use of any surplus funds; however, operator annual benefits (including stipends and other compensation) should not exceed 10% of the revenue" (Education Institute, 2004, p. 17). Operators could no longer turn all surplus funds into personal compensation. Further restrictions on surpluses were to follow. In March 2006, the Executive Committee decided that the surpluses of schools' budgets would be placed in a special account overseen by Shared Services. Funds were available on request from this account for school-related expenses, subject to approval by the Education Institute. Thus, the SEC exercised its fiscal monitoring capacity by imposing restrictions on the use of funds and placing surpluses in a holding account. Although anectodal evidence suggested that parents and other stakeholders were concerned about profit-taking on the part of operators, we found no evidence that operators received any portion of profits in 2004–2005, however, and thus we assume that the restrictions were preemptive rather than necessary to curb abuses manifest at the time (Supreme Education Council, 2006a).

We found one additional fiscal guideline in the form of salary floors for Qatari staff. The Education Institute established minimum salaries for Independent school staff members on the basis of educational level and prior service in the Ministry of Education. Staffing

[12] Only four out of 33 Generation I and II schools allocated less than 60 percent of their overall budget to instructional staff, one of which was a vocational school with a technology-intensive curriculum. Only seven out of 33 schools allocated less than 17 percent of their overall budget to administrative staff costs.

reports provide monthly salary amounts and staff members' nationality, but the reports do not note the staff members' education level to allow for monitoring a school's compliance with this requirement. Therefore, we were unable to check whether the prescribed minimum salary levels had been respected by the schools. It was also unclear whether the Finance Office could monitor these levels without relying on individuals to report departures from the minimum levels.

In addition to the above fiscal oversight activities, a measure of accountability was built into the system in the form of school choice, and this was intended to be a key new element of the reform. In theory, parents can contribute to holding schools accountable for meeting their children's educational needs by choosing the schools to which they send their children. Schools that fail to attract parents and students will not survive in the educational marketplace. Schools that survive, on the other hand, will be those whose academic and extracurricular offerings have sufficiently captured the interest of parents and students. Parents can use assessment results and other information disseminated to the public to understand how well schools perform relative to each other and make informed choices regarding where their children will attend school.

Currently, the Evaluation Institute disseminates school report cards to inform parents of the academic performance and features of every Independent, Ministry, and private Arabic school in Qatar. However, the choice mechanism is fairly weak. All Independent schools to date have been converted from Ministry schools. Many Independent schools are oversubscribed, and preference is given to students who attended the school before conversion and to students within the school's catchment area (Supreme Education Council, 2007a). In addition, space in the Independent schools is further constrained by limited facilities and requirements to limit class sizes to 25 students. These factors may result in a lack of incentive for Independent schools to achieve higher performance levels to attract enrollments. However, the fact that many Independent schools have waiting lists may encourage Ministry schools to raise their standards. One argument in favor of choice is that competition may result in positive spillover effects on conventional schools. We have no information on the incentive structures for

Ministry schools, however, and cannot assess whether spillover effects have occurred.

It can be seen from this discussion that the finance system relied primarily on spending restrictions. These restrictions appear to have been effective in achieving desired ratios for instructional and administrative expenditures. In addition, potential profit-taking among school operators appears to have been prevented. However, reducing access to surpluses may curb the flexibility of operators to make investments in high-quality education. It is unclear whether the accountability provisions established through the finance system have had a positive, negative, or neutral effect on school quality. In addition, the choice mechanism—one of the principles underlying the reform—has been relatively weak because of capacity constraints and is unlikely to have provided strong incentive to raise quality.

## Stability/Responsiveness

Compared with the traditional Ministry system, principal-operators of Independent schools have been afforded a great deal of autonomy in staff selection, pedagogical practice, and resource allocation. To make long-term investments in high-quality staffing, curricula, and facilities, however, a reliable flow of funding is needed. Furthermore, by providing sustained support to school operators, the reform's leaders promote a sense of trust in the system among operators.

In addition to fostering a sense of predictability, however, a sound finance system must also be flexible to address changing needs or goals within the system or problems as they arise. It is therefore necessary to conduct ongoing needs assessments to ascertain whether changes in funding policies are necessary. For example, analyses can be undertaken to determine whether cost-of-living changes warrant adjustments to staff salaries or whether technology infrastructure improvements warrant adjustments to per-pupil allotments.

In short, the finance system must strike a helpful balance between *stability* and *responsiveness*. Stability refers to a predictable operating environment that allows school operators to establish both long- and short-term strategies for improving their schools, and responsiveness indicates an ability of the governing body to intervene and fine-tune the reform.

We found that in the early years of the school finance system supporting the K–12 reform in Qatar, the balance between stability and responsiveness tilted heavily toward the latter. Changes to finance-related policies were frequently instituted as financial and administrative information on the Independent schools flowed in, and measures were taken to address perceived problems in the system.

The existence of substantial surpluses and the desire to promote Qatari nationals in leadership positions formed the impetus for funding cutbacks and changes in regulations guiding the reform. These changes took the form of added restrictions on surplus accumulation and operator compensation (described in the previous section), the elimination of grants as an added source of funding, and a change in the legal status and leadership requirements for the schools, including requirements that operators be Qatari nationals and serve as principals of the schools.

To promote a variety of schooling options for students, the original reform design allowed any individuals or groups from the community to apply for the position of school operator, subject to the approval of the SEC. For example, a group of parents could unite to start an Independent school or Qatar Petroleum could open a school that emphasized science and mathematics to provide a potential source of future talent for the company. As mentioned above, the first Independent schools were privately incorporated as LLCs. At least two people are needed to form an LLC in Qatar, and one must be Qatari. Therefore, teams of operators formed. By virtue of their status as LLCs, schools became for-profit entities. As of March 2006, however, regulations regarding operators and legal entities changed: Independent schools must now be nonprofits and an operator must now be a Qatari national and also be the school's principal (Supreme Education Council, 2006b).

In addition to these policy shifts, the SEC made policy decisions affecting resource use in Independent schools. In May 2005, the SEC set minimum salaries for Qatari educators (Supreme Education Council, 2005), and in October 2005, the SEC specified that the use of surplus funds be directed toward meeting Qatarization goals (Education Institute, 2005). Before this—in the first year of operation of Generation I Independent schools—operators had the freedom to recruit teachers from whichever countries they wanted to fulfill teaching and staffing needs, provided they adjusted their budget accordingly and took into consideration their per-pupil-allotment funding. For example, five of the 12 Independent schools opened in 2004 used English as the language of instruction and wanted to therefore rely on teachers whose native language was English. It was expected that these teachers would be more expensive because of their language abilities.

After the first year of Independent school operation, however, the Qatarization policy described in the introduction to this monograph was put in place to promote the hiring of Qatari nationals in schools. The policy set quotas for the employment of Qataris within each school. The quotas differed by level and type of school in recognition of the different balances of Qataris and expatriate teachers needed for boys and girls at different ages and ranged from 20 percent in boys' secondary schools to 70 percent in girls' secondary schools (Supreme Education Council, 2005). The Qatarization requirements are illustrated in Table 3.2.

In addition to the establishment of Qatarization goals, a 40 percent increase in the base salary of Qatari nationals in the Civil Service was instituted in September 2007 in response to nationwide increases in the cost of living, driven largely by increases in the price of real estate. Many Qatari teachers in Independent schools were classified as Civil Service employees.[13] To furnish the funds for the mandated salary

---

[13] Full-time Qatari employees "seconded" (i.e., transferred) from any Ministry in Qatar remain part of the Qatar Civil Service Cadre and therefore are entitled to a basic salary not less than the basic salary they were entitled to before. In addition to the basic monthly salaries for Qatari employees who remain part of the Civil Service Cadre, from 2004–2006 they were entitled to the same allowances as employees holding similar posts on the Civil Service Cadre (Education Institute, 2004). As of 2006–2007, the Education Institute also listed specific amounts for allowances that schools must pay their Qatari staff, whether directly hired or seconded. This list included a social allowance for single and for married employees, a housing allowance to married employees, and a transportation allowance (Supreme Education Council, 2007c).

**Table 3.2**
**Qatarization Requirements in Independent Schools**

| School Type | Percentage of Qatari Staff |
|---|---|
| Girls | |
| Primary | 70 |
| Preparatory | 60 |
| Secondary | 60 |
| Boys | |
| Primary model | 70 |
| Primary | 30 |
| Preparatory | 25 |
| Secondary | 20 |

SOURCE: Supreme Education Council (2005).

increases, the SEC increased per-pupil allotments by QR 2,000 for all primary schools and by QR 1,000 for preparatory girls' and secondary girls' schools, beginning in 2007–2008 (Supreme Education Council, 2007d). These increases are meant to "encourage more Qatari involvement in the reform initiative" and "ensure that Qatari staff in independent schools enjoy the same living standards as their partners in other official sectors" (Supreme Education Council, 2007b). These changes, in addition to the elimination of grants in 2005–2006 and the elimination of start-up funds for new schools in 2007–2008 (described above) represent important modifications to revenue policies. To analyze the effect of meeting Qatarization requirements and mandated salary increases, we built a forecasting tool that modeled changes in the system and translated them into projected expenditure estimates for the reform as a whole and for specific sectors within the reform (Armstrong, 2001). The forecasting tool and the projected implications of the policy changes are discussed in detail in the next chapter.

Most of the changes to the system that we have described above have represented early adjustments as information on school finance became available for the first time. As a result of the many changes, however, operators and principals may have lacked the stability needed to plan effectively for long-term investments in the educational process. Also, some of the policy changes implemented ran counter to the reform principals of autonomy, accountability, variety, and choice. It remains to be seen whether stability in the reform's finance system will grow over time and allow school leaders to gain familiarity with the structure and plan effectively.

## Summary/Conclusions

We evaluated the progress of the funding system as of the end of the 2005–2006 school year against six objectives that characterize a highly functioning school finance system: transparency, equity, adequacy, efficiency, accountability, and stability/responsiveness. Despite the fact that we identify several areas for improvement, the system was new at the time of our evaluation and achieved a noteworthy degree of success in supporting a growing reform through its early stages. Our evaluation can be summarized as follows:

- *Transparency.* Although the finance system improved in its transparency over the two years under consideration in this monograph, a number of issues pertaining to the quality and accessibility of data need further attention. The data-reporting system in place during the period covered by this evaluation is currently being replaced by a new management information system, which, it is hoped, will address the following issues:
  - Data were often incomplete and lacking in comparability across entities and time periods.
  - Data were often difficult to access and did not always contain the amount of detail necessary for a complete analysis. Many data were not available electronically and had to be manually entered into electronic spreadsheets that could then be ana-

lyzed. Some data did not contain standardized categories, which would have greatly facilitated accurate analysis.

- *Equity.* We compared per-pupil expenditures in girls' and boys' schools.
  - Girls' and boys' schools did not differ substantially in per-pupil spending in the small number of schools in the analysis sample. However, the apparent parity masked underlying differences in the salary structures in the two types of schools, which reflect inequities in the Qatari labor market. Male teachers earned more than female teachers, and Qatari teachers earned more than non-Qatari teachers. Boys' schools employed greater proportions of male teachers but smaller proportions of Qatari teachers than girls' schools did. Thus, spending on different groups of teachers in boys' and girls' schools tended to offset the differences, and overall parity was apparently achieved through the staffing mix.
- *Adequacy.* We approached the question of determining adequacy in funding levels by developing a "successful schools" method and applying it to the limited data currently available in the system. We developed measures of school performance that adjusted for the prior performance and demographic characteristics of students and found the following:
  - Our analyses suggest that a positive relationship exists between higher per-pupil spending and primary school performance on standardized tests in Arabic, English, and mathematics and between fewer pupils per teacher and primary school performance on standardized tests in Arabic and English. Results are preliminary, however, because of the small number of schools currently in the system and must be interpreted as merely suggestive. Expansion of the reform in future years will support more powerful analyses that should be able to detect relationships between test score outcomes and resource use and to suggest target levels for funding and other resources.
  - Ultimately, the successful schools method relies on the existence of defined levels of student proficiency. Such performance standards have not yet been established in Qatar. If the

higher-performing schools are operating at the desired level of excellence, our analysis suggests that current funding levels may be adequate at the primary school level. If they are not, then spending in these schools might be insufficient and per-pupil allocations may be inadequate. Thus, in the absence of clear performance goals, even the successful schools method is limited in its ability to capture a notion of funding adequate to support excellence in education.

- *Efficiency.* We currently lack the data necessary to assess the efficiency of the system. More Independent schools are needed at each level and several must be high-performing schools before solid conclusions may be drawn.
- *Accountability.* We attempted to evaluate the finance system's use of two types of accountability mechanisms: fiscal oversight and parental choice.
  - Accountability was exercised in the form of fiscal monitoring. This was particularly evident in the number and type of restrictions placed on the use of surpluses. Fiscal requirements were, by and large, adhered to by all schools.
  - Parental choice was only partially operating in the 2004–2005 and 2005-2006 years and does not appear to have provided incentive for schools to raise performance levels.
- *Stability/responsiveness.* We evaluated the system's responsiveness in enacting changes against whether it provided enough financial stability to allow for planning and investment.
  - The system introduced several changes to regulations governing the financing of the Independent schools between 2004 and 2006.
  - It was particularly responsive to evidence that surplus funds had accumulated by introducing funding cutbacks and restrictions on the use of funds.
  - However, as a result of the many changes, in our view, operators and principals may have lacked the stability needed to plan effectively for investments in the educational process.

CHAPTER FOUR

# Tool to Forecast Spending on the Reform

To provide a useful tool to further the SEC's ability to monitor and modify financial flows to the reform, we built a causal forecasting model to project future expenditures on Independent schools and overall reform under different scenarios. Education planning efforts have long relied on forecasting tools, dating back to the late 18th and early 19th centuries (Coombs, 1970).

Generally, forecasting models may be categorized across three dimensions: (1) the type of process to be modeled (judgmental or statistical), (2) the type of information sources available (single- or multisource, uni- or multivariate), and (3) the role that theory or actors play in the forecasting model, if any (Armstrong, 2001). As such, there is a broad range of analytic techniques classified generally as forecasting models.[1] For the phenomenon we are trying to forecast (expenditures on Qatar's education reform), the modeling environment has sufficient objective data to create a mathematical model, good knowledge of relationships between the dependent and independent variables (how expenditures are driven ultimately by the number of pupils or the number of schools), and information on potentially large changes in portions of the current system. These conditions led us to adopt what is

[1] Methods include the Delphi method or prediction markets, judgmental bootstrapping, conjoint analysis, intentions or expectations of decisionmakers, role-playing, structured analogies, quantitative analogies, expert systems, rule-based forecasting, extrapolation or data mining, and causal models. Each of these types of forecasting methods has a large, well-developed literature associated with it. See Armstrong (2001) for explanations of these types of methods.

generally termed a "causal model" with elements of an "extrapolation model."

Causal models relate a dependent variable to various causal variables based on a specified theory, prior research, or expert domain knowledge (Armstrong, 2001). Here we use the given relationship between the amount of funding schools receive and the number of students at each level. In the previous chapters, we saw that primary, preparatory, and secondary school per-pupil allocations are specified by policy. Thus, using reasonable assumptions for growth in the number of schools and the number of students, we can forecast total expenditures on per-pupil allotments.

Extrapolation models assume that past behavior is a good predictor of future behavior (Armstrong, 2001). However, they assume that nothing is relevant other than prior values. Accordingly, we combine the projection principle in extrapolation models with the allowance for change in causal models. In our model, we know the principal expenditure drivers (pupils) but make assumptions regarding growth rates of pupils. Although the number of pupils grows as a causal forecast, costs per pupil differ with the policy levers of Qatarization and wage increases. We decompose the model into constituent types of expenditure, including per-pupil allocations, start-up costs, grants, and differences in Independent schools and various institutions and assets. We explicitly model fixed and variable costs. We model five alternatives to explore differences in cost for various policy choices of Qatarization and wages. As with all forecasting models, there is no way to describe future states with complete certainty. Still, this model provides policymakers with useful insights in formulating policy around the reform.

We wish to emphasize that our aim is not to provide accurate forecasts of expenditures on the Independent school system or the reform as a whole. Rather, we present a tool that can be used to forecast expenditures and model the effect of policy changes. The model provided in this chapter includes our rough understanding of proposed and already implemented policy, but clearly its assumptions need to be refined. For example, accurate forecasting must include an assessment of the effect of particular policies, including the likelihood that proposed policy will successfully be implemented. Such refined analyses can be conducted using the data available to decisionmakers and policymakers at the SEC, which will make it unnecessary to rely on the strong assumptions made here.

This model is constructed for Qatar's K–12 reform, and many elements are specific to the country and to the nature of its reform. Nevertheless the methodology can be employed more generally in environments where objective data and good knowledge of relationships between the dependent and independent variables exists. In particular, the forecasting tool is useful in contexts where there is a rapid transformation of the education system from one type of system to another.

## Forecasting Tool

Our forecasting tool is composed of four parts:

1. The first part predicts the total expenditures on the reform, based on total school operating revenues, contract costs, asset procurement costs, and institute costs
2. The second part predicts total costs for contracts, asset procurement, or institutes
3. The third part predicts total school operating revenues
4. The last part predicts per-pupil allocations for each type of Independent school.

A set of inputs can be varied to determine the effect of various policies. The policy levers that can be manipulated at different points in time to produce different cost scenarios are the following:

- number of Independent schools—i.e., the schedule for conversion from Ministry schools and any start-up Independent schools
- average student enrollment per school over time, by school level and school gender
- per-pupil allocations over time, by school level and school gender
- start-up funding and grants per school over time

- growth rates in variable and fixed costs of contracts, assets, and institutes
- teacher-pupil ratios over time, by school level and school gender
- Qatarization percentages over time, by teacher gender, school level, and school gender
- staff salaries over time, by teacher gender, teacher nationality, school level, and school gender.

In addition to these policy levers, the models incorporate assumptions based on outside information regarding population growth rates of primary, preparatory, and secondary school populations.

The model itself consists of a set of interactive Excel spreadsheets. Once the inputs are entered, the model calculates the various types of costs. Outputs consist of both the raw numbers and charts showing the trajectory of expenditures over time. Below, we describe each part of the model and the inputs that feed into it in a series of simplified schematic diagrams. Then, we use the actual model to predict total expenditures and output charts under different scenarios.

Figure 4.1 shows a schematic representation of the major components of expenditures on the reform, as described in Chapter Two: school operating expenditures, contracts, assets, and institutes. We model each of these four components separately, given their different dynamics. We first discuss the component that models school operating revenues, the largest expenditure component of the Independent school system (left-hand side of Figure 4.1).

Figure 4.2 shows in more detail the modeling of school operating revenues, consisting of per-pupil operating income, start-up funding and operating grants. The most important determinants of expenditures on the reform in the model are the total number of schools and the average number of students in each school, by school level and school gender. Per-pupil operating income, for example, is driven by the total number of students, by school level, multiplied by the per-pupil allotments (which differ by school level and school gender), whereas total start-up funding is driven by the number of schools that have recently been converted to Independent schools (number of schools added). Given that miscellaneous income is not a source of revenue provided

**Figure 4.1**
**Schematic Representation of the Four Major Components of Expenditures on Independent Schools Under the Reform**

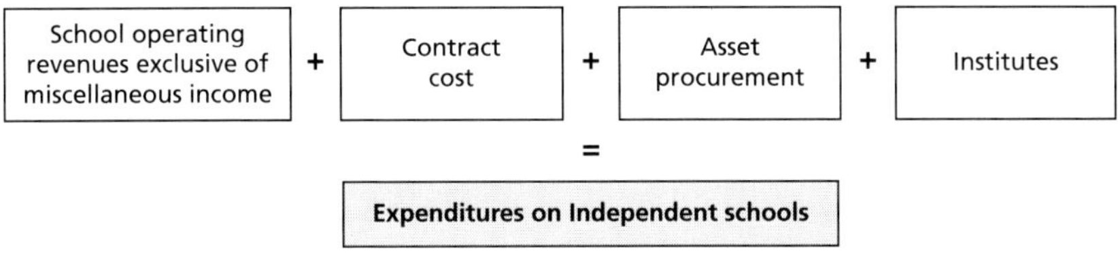


RAND *MG839-4.1*

**Figure 4.2**
**Schematic Representation of the School Operating Revenue Forecast**

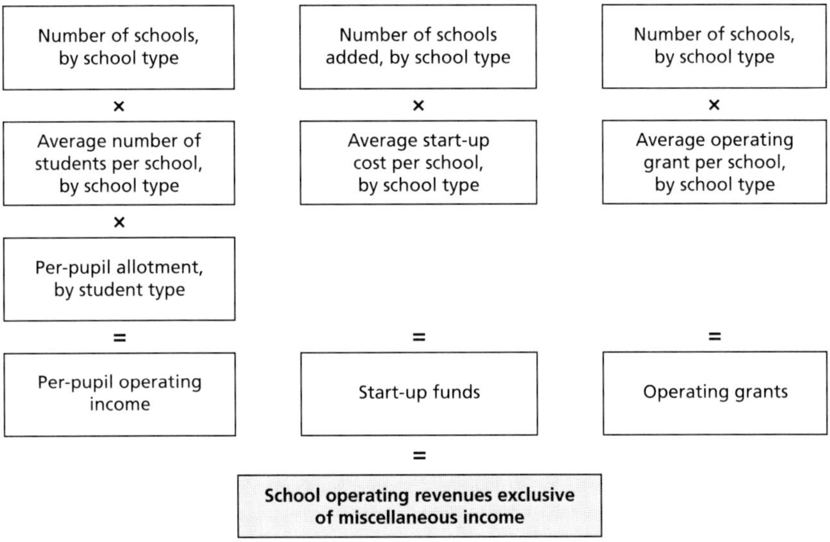


RAND *MG839-4.2*

by the SEC and is therefore not a cost component of the reform, it is not included in the modeling.

An added benefit to relying on the total number of schools and average number of students per school by school level and school gender as the main driver of the model is that, over time, there is a relatively high degree of certainty regarding these figures. Under the assumption that all Ministry schools will eventually convert to Independent schools over a specified time period (the anticipated date is by 2012–2013), we know how many schools and students likely still need to be converted. The number of conversions to be made each year remains uncertain, however, and must be assumed to predict the trajectory of expenditures over the forecast period.

An essential element of school operating revenue is the per-pupil allotment (third box in the left hand column of Figure 4.2). We forecast per-pupil allocations by assuming that they follow the same trend as operating expenditures per pupil.[2] Figure 4.3 shows schematically how operating revenues and expenditures for each school level and school gender are modeled. The model is based primarily on staffing expenditures, the largest component of overall expenditures.

As Figure 4.3 shows, the three components of expenditures used to forecast per-pupil allocations are teacher wages, administrative wages, and nonwage-related expenditures. As discussed in Chapter Two, administrative and instructional wages account for about 85 percent of total expenditures, and administrative wages account for about 25 percent of total wage expenditures. We have used these ratios as our starting point but subsequently allow for differences in growth of each type of expenditure.

In the first year of operation of Independent schools, operators had the freedom to recruit teachers from whichever countries they wanted to fulfill their teaching and staffing needs, provided they adjusted their budget accordingly and took into consideration their per-pupil-allotment funding. In subsequent years, policies to promote the hiring of Qatari nationals in schools (i.e., Qatarization), and to set minimum salaries for Qataris, were put into place in an effort to encourage operators to hire more Qataris and to attract more Qataris to apply for teaching positions in Independent schools (Supreme Education Council, 2005). Table 3.3 shows Qatarization requirements by school level.

The potential effect of enforcing Qatarization quotas can be modeled by changing the mix in the nationality of teachers. The effect of wage increases, such as the impending 40 percent increase in the base

---

[2] If they do not follow the same trend and expenditures rise faster than per-pupil allocations, schools may begin to face deficits. It is likely that corrective action will be taken in such cases to ensure that per-pupil allocations track per-pupil expenditures.

**Figure 4.3**
**Schematic Representation of the Per-Pupil Allocation Forecast**

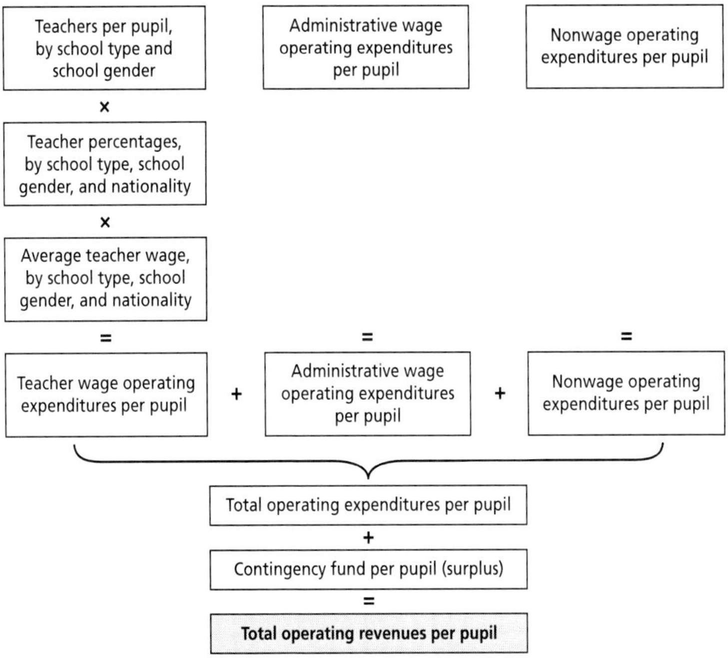


RAND *MG839-4.3*

salaries of Qatari staff in 2006–2007, is modeled by varying teacher wages for each school type (level and gender), teacher gender, and teacher nationality.[3]

We sum the three components of operating expenditures and allow for a certain percentage of revenues to be set aside for contingency funding. We then apply the implied increase in revenues to the

---

[3] From staffing report data on the ratio of base to total salary for Qatari teachers, we estimate the following increases in total salaries resulting from the 40 percent increase in base salary: boys' model, 25.9 percent; boys' primary, N/A; girls' primary, 24.6 percent; boys' preparatory, 17.6 percent; girls' preparatory, 23.6 percent; boys' secondary, 14.2 percent; girls' secondary, N/A. Because salary data on both base and total salary were not available for all schools, we do not have information on the ratio of base to total salary for boys' primary schools and for girls' secondary schools. Using these observations, we make the simplifying assumption that female-taught schools experience a 25 percent increase in total salary costs and male-taught schools a 16 percent increase for Qatari teachers as a result of the mandated 40 percent increase in base salary.

per-pupil allocations for each school level and school gender (boys' versus girls' schools) using 2005–2006 as the base year.

The output of this model—the forecast of per-pupil allocations by school level and school gender—is input to the forecasts of the aggregate operating income from per-pupil funding (the third box on the left hand side of Figure 4.2) and is the final piece needed to provide the forecast for school revenues (the first box on the left-hand side of Figure 4.1).

Figure 4.4 shows how the remaining three expenditure components of the reform, contracts, assets, and institutes, are modeled (the remaining three boxes to the right in Figure 4.1). As Figure 4.4 shows, costs are separated into variable costs (those costs that vary with the number of schools or the number of students) and fixed costs (those that do not). Some examples of possible fixed costs include office space rent, furniture, accounting services, and payroll services for the institutes and administrative services associated with asset procurement. Possible variable costs include salaries of staff at the institutes,

**Figure 4.4**
**Schematic Representation of the Cost of Contracts (C), Asset Procurement (AP), or Institutes (I) Forecasts**

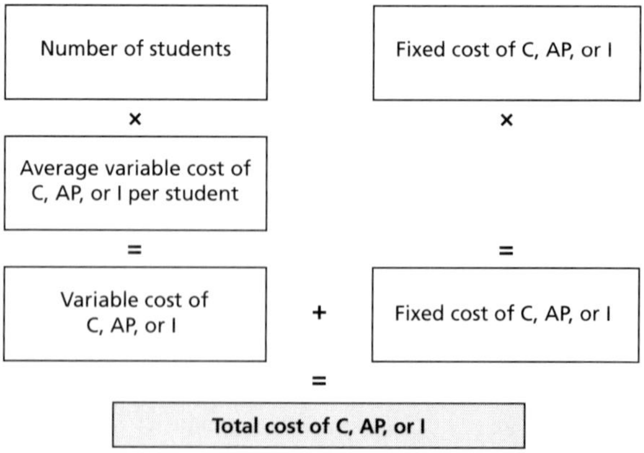


NOTES: The method of forecast is the same for each of these three cost components. Variable costs are costs that vary as a function of the number of schools; fixed costs do *not* vary with the number of schools. Variable costs can also be expressed per student instead of per school.

RAND *MG839-4.4*

equipment and material provided to Independent schools, Independent schools' asset maintenance, and contracts for external auditing of Independent schools.

This part of the model is the least developed. Our determination of fixed and variable costs relies on very little historical information, essentially the 2004–2005 and 2005–2006 years. The model can be improved by incorporating additional data from subsequent years and carefully assessing those costs that are fixed and those that are variable. For now, the model estimates serve to illustrate the potential for forecasting these costs, but forecasts of the costs of contracts, assets, and institutes should not be considered robust based on the information currently available.

## Model Scenarios

For illustrative purposes, we use the forecasting model to predict total expenditures under five scenarios corresponding to proposed or impending policy changes. These scenarios are presented in Table 4.1. Note that scenario E represents the situation in which all policy changes that have been proposed as of the end of 2007 are implemented.

In addition to the assumptions presented for the scenarios A to E we assume the following for each of the scenarios:

- population growth in line with Census forecasts of the primary, preparatory, and secondary school populations
- a constant average student population per school for each school level and school gender[4]
- discontinuation of start-up funding and grants[5]
- no growth in the fixed and the variable costs (real QR) of contracts, asset procurement, and institutes

---

[4] The assumption is that in the conversion from Ministry to Independent schools, smaller Ministry schools are merged into the larger format of Independent schools.

[5] We assumed that one school, a vocational school with a technology-intensive curriculum, will continue to be funded through operating grants, but that no other schools will receive operating grants in the future.

**Table 4.1**
**Model Scenarios**

| Scenario | School Conversion by 2012–2013 | 40% Base Salary Increase for Qatari Teachers in 2006–2007 | Annual (Real) % Salary Increase for Teachers | Qatarization Goals Achieved by 2015–2016 | Description |
|---|---|---|---|---|---|
| A | No | Yes | 0 | No | After cohort IV (2007–2008) no new schools are converted. |
| B | Yes | No | 0 | No | Per-pupil allocations are not adjusted for the additional expenditures related to salary increases. |
| C | Yes | Yes | 0 | No | Per-pupil allocations are adjusted for the additional expenditures related to the 40 percent base salary increase for Qatari teachers in 2006–2007. |
| D | Yes | Yes | 3 | No | Per-pupil allocations are adjusted for the additional expenditures related to the 40 percent base salary increase for Qatari teachers in 2006–2007, as well as a 3 percent annual real salary increase for all teachers. Qatarization is assumed to remain constant. |
| E | Yes | Yes | 3 | Yes | Per-pupil allocations are adjusted for the additional expenditures related to the 40 percent base salary increase for Qatari teachers in 2006–2007, as well as a 3 percent annual real salary increase for all teachers. The Qatarization goals set are reached by 2015. |

SOURCES: Finance Office; KPMG; RAND analysis.

NOTES: We do not assume that the 40 percent salary raise for Qatari staff did not occur; instead we assume here that per-pupil allocations are not adjusted to compensate schools for the additional expenses. Real wages per pupil (after correcting for an annual inflation rate of 2.4 percent reported by Qatar Central Bank) grew, on average, by 4.1 percent per year for Ministry schools between 1995 and 2005 (RAND analysis of Ministry of Education average wage information). If teachers-per-pupil ratios remained constant over the period, the 4.1 percent wages per-pupil increase is reflective of the wage increase for teachers. Conservatively, to allow for some change in the teachers-per-pupil ratio, we use 3 percent annual wage increases.

- constant teacher per-pupil ratios for each school level and school gender
- initial total wages as 85 percent of operating expenses
- a ratio of administrative to instructional wages of 25 percent
- a constant allowance for contingency funding of 10 percent
- growth in administrative real wage expenditures of 3 percent per year
- growth in real nonwage operating expenditures of 3 percent per year.

All forecasts are presented in real QR based on the 2005–2006 value of the currency (i.e., we do not adjust our projections to include inflation in the value of the QR). Therefore, growth rates in the model should be interpreted as rates above inflation (real growth).

The model uses as its starting point the information reported in Chapter Two for both the 2004–2005 and 2005–2006 operating years.[6] To restrict ourselves to estimating expenditures on the K–12 reform only, we excluded the Higher Education Institute by reducing the 2005–2006 total amount spent on the institutes by 16 percent (this is the percentage spent on the Higher Education Institute over the period July 2005 to March 2006—the only time period for which this information was available).

Figures 4.5 through 4.9 show forecasts of expenditures on the Independent school system under the different scenarios. In any of the following forecasting scenarios, Ministry spending before the K–12 reform was announced in 2002 may serve as a useful benchmark for comparison. The Ministry reported total spending of 1.61 billion QR on K–12 education (nominal QR), which corresponds to 22,249 QR on a per-pupil basis, for the 2001–2002 school year (Ministry of Education, 2005).

---

[6] This includes information on the costs of institutes, assets, and contracts from Finance Office data, the cost of operations of Independent schools from KPMG and Deloitte & Touche financial statements (including per-pupil funding, start-up funding and grants, but excluding miscellaneous income), and staff salaries and the number of teachers by gender and nationality for each type of school from the Finance Office (see Appendix A for more details).

**Figure 4.5**
**Forecast of Expenditures on the Reform, Scenario A**

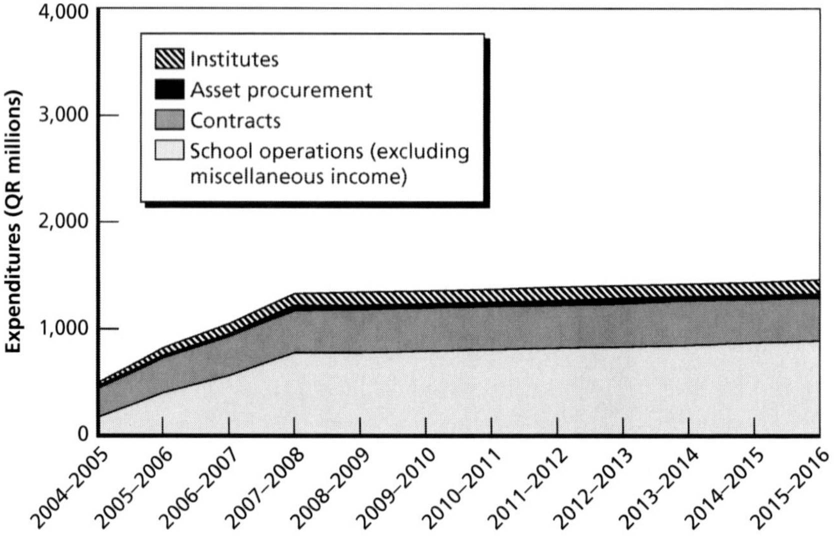


RAND *MG839-4.5*

Under scenario A, there is no further growth in the number of Independent schools after 2007–2008, resulting in substantially slower growth in expenditures. The increase in total expenditures after 2007–2008 is due to (i) growth of the primary, preparatory, and secondary school populations in line with Census forecasts (between 0 percent and 2 percent per year), (ii) growth in administrative real wage expenditures of 3 percent per year, and (iii) growth in real nonwage operating expenditures of 3 percent per year.

Under scenario B, per-pupil allocations are not adjusted for the additional expenditures related to salary increases, i.e., they remain constant (in real QR). Growth in expenditures is primarily due to growth in the number of students and schools as the conversion of Ministry schools to Independent schools is continued. Conversion is completed by 2012–2013, after which growth is due to the same four factors as in scenario A after 2007–2008.

Under scenario C, per-pupil allocations are adjusted for the additional expenditures related to the 40 percent base salary increase in

**Figure 4.6**
**Forecast of Expenditures on the Reform, Scenario B**

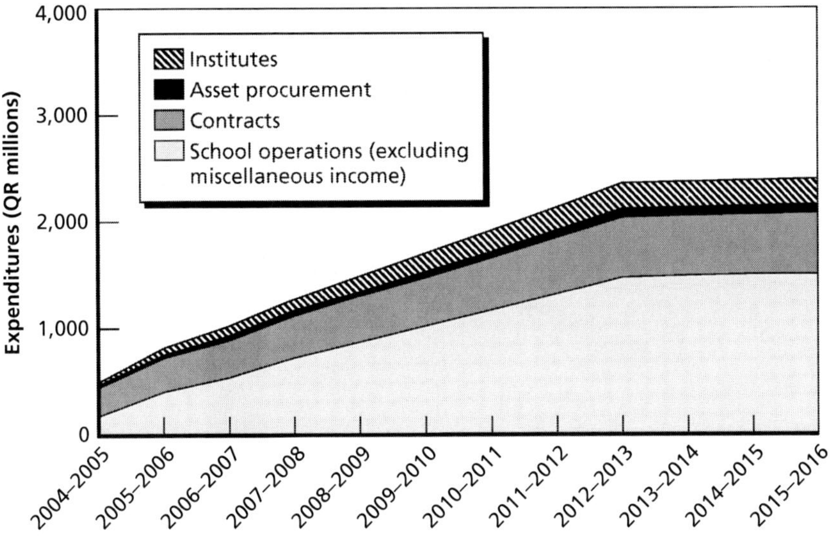


RAND *MG839-4.6*

2006–2007 for Qatari personnel. As in scenario B, growth in expenditures is primarily due to growth in the number of students and schools as the conversion of Ministry schools to Independent schools is continued. But, total expenditures are about 10 percent higher because of the 40 percent base salary increase in 2006–2007 for Qatari personnel. Conversion is completed by 2012–2013, after which growth is due to the same four factors as in scenario A after 2007–2008.

Under scenario D, per-pupil allocations are adjusted for the additional expenditures related to the 40 percent base salary increase in 2006–2007 for Qatari personnel, as well as a 3 percent annual real salary increase[7] for all personnel. As in scenarios B and C, growth in expenditures is primarily due to growth in the number of students and schools as the conversion of Ministry schools to Independent schools is continued. But, total expenditures are about 12 percent higher than

---

[7] Real wages (corrected for inflation) grew on average by 4.1 percent for Ministry schools between 1995 and 2005.

**Figure 4.7**
**Forecast of Expenditures on the Reform, Scenario C**

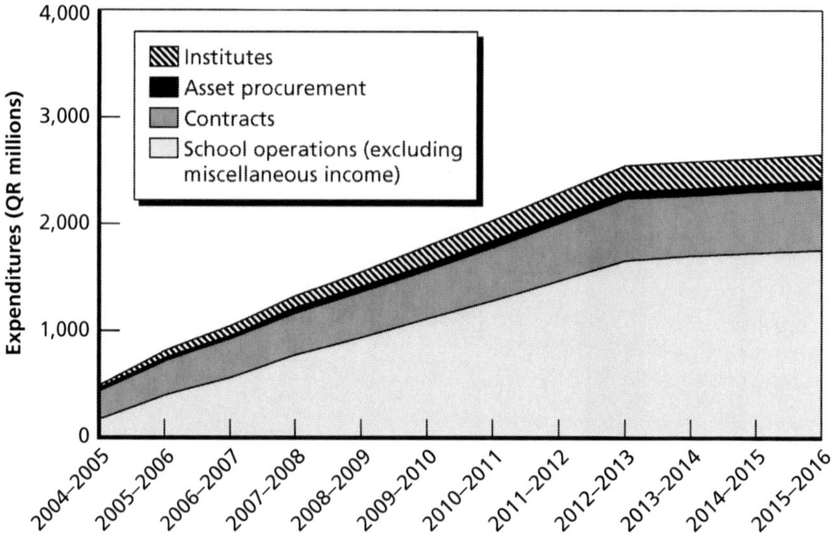


RAND *MG839-4.7*

in scenario C because of the additional 3 percent average annual salary increase for all personnel. Conversion is completed by 2012–2013, after which growth is due to the same four factors as in scenario A after 2007–2008.

Under scenario E, per-pupil allocations are adjusted for the additional expenditures related to the 40 percent base salary increase in 2006–2007 for Qatari personnel, as well as a 3 percent annual real salary increase for all personnel. As in scenarios B, C, and D, growth in expenditures is primarily due to growth in the number of students and schools as the conversion of Ministry schools to Independent schools is continued. But, total expenditures are about 5 percent higher than in scenario D as the Qatarization goals are fully achieved by 2015. Conversion is completed by 2012–2013, after which growth is due to the same four factors as in scenario A after 2007–2008.

**Figure 4.8**
**Forecast of Expenditures on the Reform, Scenario D**

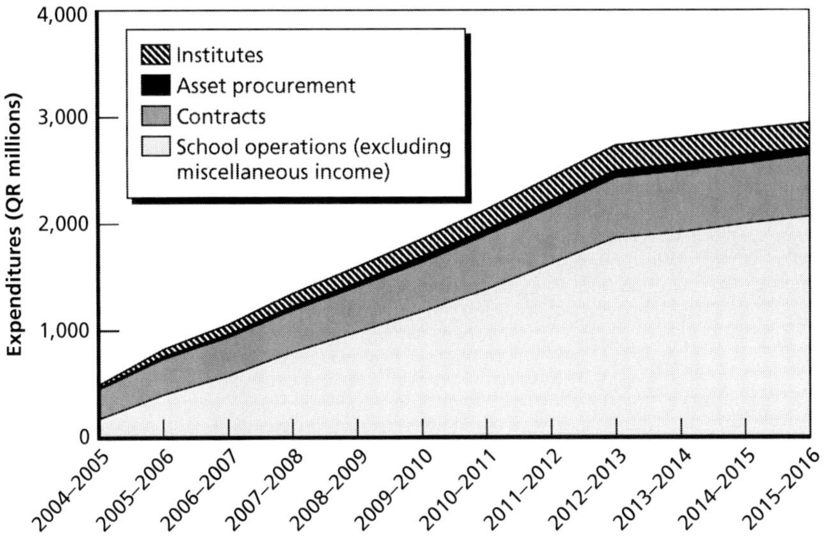


RAND *MG839-4.8*

## Per-Pupil Allocations

Figure 4.10 provides a brief summary of the forecasted per-pupil allocations (again in real QR) for scenarios A through E for the year 2015–2016. Scenario B functions as a reference to 2005–2006; in scenario B, per-pupil allocations remain constant (in real terms) and hence remain at their 2005–2006 level. Scenarios A and C are equivalent in their per-pupil allocations; the main difference between the two scenarios is the number of students and schools in the Independent schools system. Given that per-pupil allocations are on a per-pupil basis, the forecasted per-pupil allocations are exactly the same. The growth in per-pupil allocations is due to (i) the 40 percent base salary increase in 2006–2007 for Qatari personnel, (ii) growth in administrative real wage expenditures of 3 percent per year, and (iii) growth in real nonwage operating expenditures of 3 percent per year. Moving

**Figure 4.9**
**Forecast of Expenditures on the Reform, Scenario E**

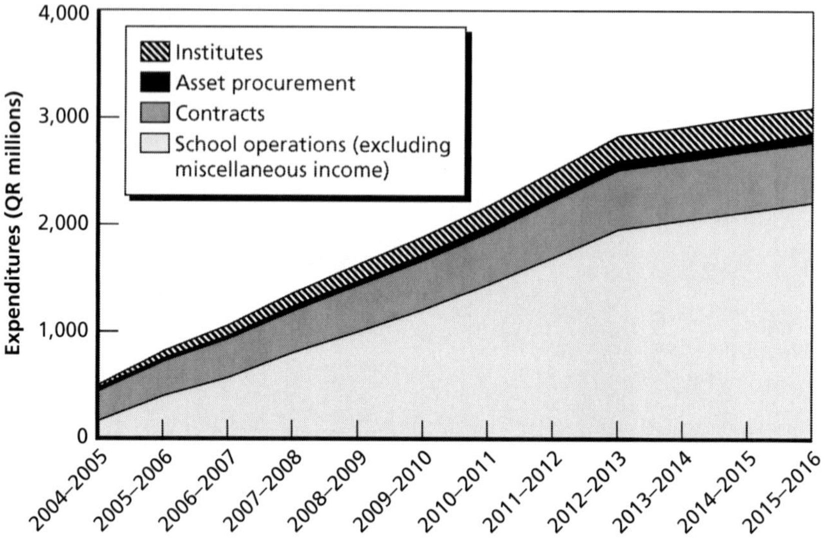


RAND *MG839-4.9*

from scenario C to D to E, the per-pupil allocations increase as a result of accounting for a 3 percent real salary increase per year for all personnel (C to D) and increases resulting from Qatarization (D to E).

Figures 4.11–4.13 show the relative effect on school expenditures of the 40 percent base salary increase for Qatari personnel in 2006–2007 as well as the effect of reaching the Qatarization goals.[8] Female-taught schools have higher percentages of Qatari nationals than do male-taught schools and are thus affected more by this salary increase. As Figure 4.11 shows, female-taught schools can expect between 5 percent and 8 percent increases in operating expenditures as

---

[8] The figure is obtained by comparing the per-pupil allocations in model E and those in model D with the results of a model that does not incorporate the 40 percent salary increase for Qatari personnel in 2006–2007 and keeps the percentage of Qatari teachers fixed. Although we have used the model to obtain these figures, the results apply more generally, as we kept constant all variables other than wages and the degree of Qatarization. The results, thus, effectively assume only a 40 percent salary increase for Qatari personnel and that Qatarization is fully achieved.

**Figure 4.10**
**Forecast of Per-Pupil Allocations Under Scenarios A through E, by School Type**

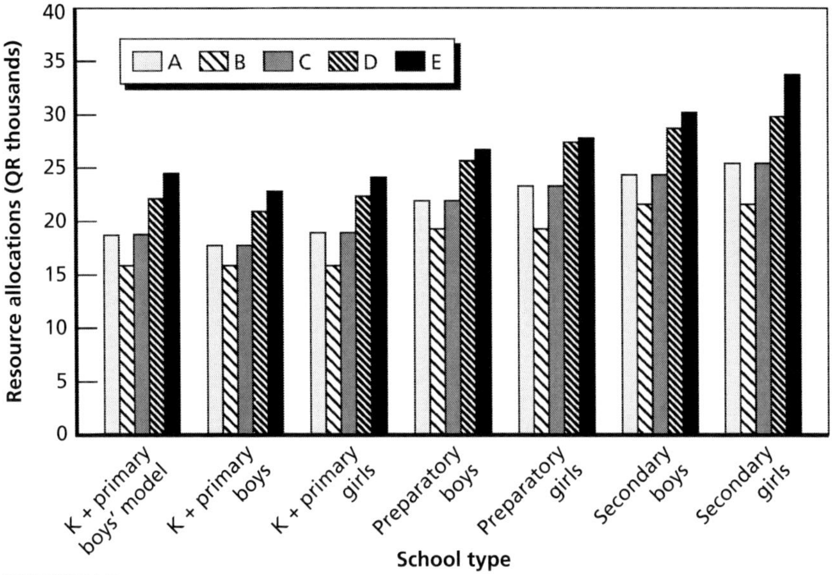


RAND *MG839-4.10*

a result of the 40 percent base salary increase for Qatari personnel in 2006–2007. This compares with between 0 percent and 1.5 percent for male-taught schools.

The per-pupil allotments were increased in 2007–2008 to QR 18,000 (12.5 percent increase) for primary schools (all types), QR 20,400 (5.2 percent) for girls' preparatory schools and QR 22,800 (4.6 percent) for girls' secondary schools. Allocations will remain at QR 19,400 for boys' preparatory schools and QR 21,800 for boys' secondary schools (Supreme Education Council, 2007d). Focusing on the near term, we assess the effect of the 40 percent base salary increase[9] and compare this with the proposed increases in per-pupil allotments (see Figure 4.12). Our analysis suggests that the net effect represent gains (indicated by plusses in Figure 4.12) in total revenues for boys' primary model, boys' primary, and girls' primary schools (of about 6, 12, and

[9] Qatarization quotas have an effect on school finances over the longer term.

**Figure 4.11**
**Percentage Increase in School Expenditures Resulting from Qatari Personnel Wage Increase, by School Type**

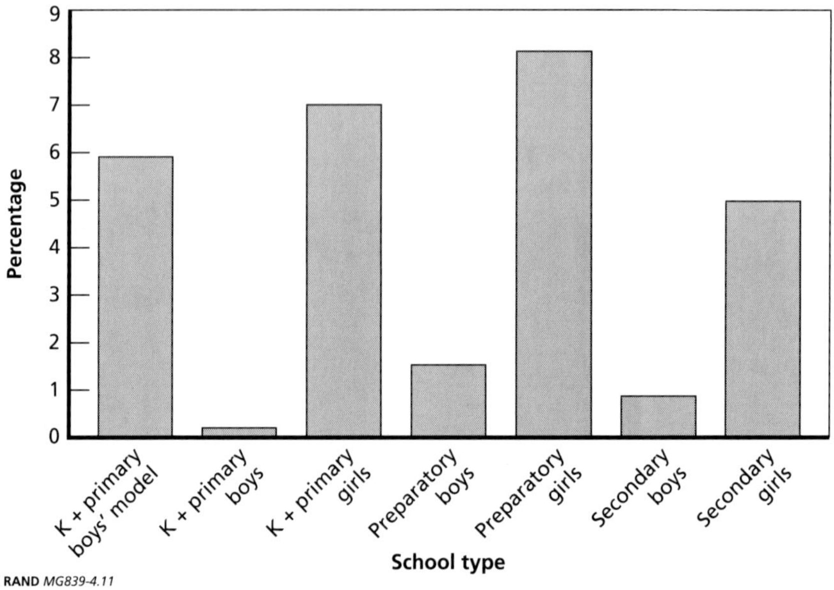


RAND *MG839-4.11*

5 percent, respectively) and losses (indicated by minuses) for boys' and girls' preparatory and boys' and girls' secondary schools (of about 2, 3, 1, and 0.5 percent, respectively). In other words, for some schools, the slated increases in per-pupil allotments will most likely not cover the increased expenditures because of the 40 percent base salary increase for Qatari staff, whereas for others, they cover expenditures more than sufficiently.

Qatarization, on the other hand, has different gender-related effects at different levels (see Figure 4.13). Girls' secondary schools would experience a much larger increase in expenditures than would boys' secondary schools, but the opposite relationship is true for girls' and boys' preparatory schools. The increases in operating expenditures from Qatarization range widely, between less than 2 percent for girls' preparatory schools and 14 percent for girls' secondary schools.

**Figure 4.12**
**Percentage Increase in School Expenditures Resulting from Qatari Staff Wage Increase and Increase in Per-Pupil Allocation, by School Type**

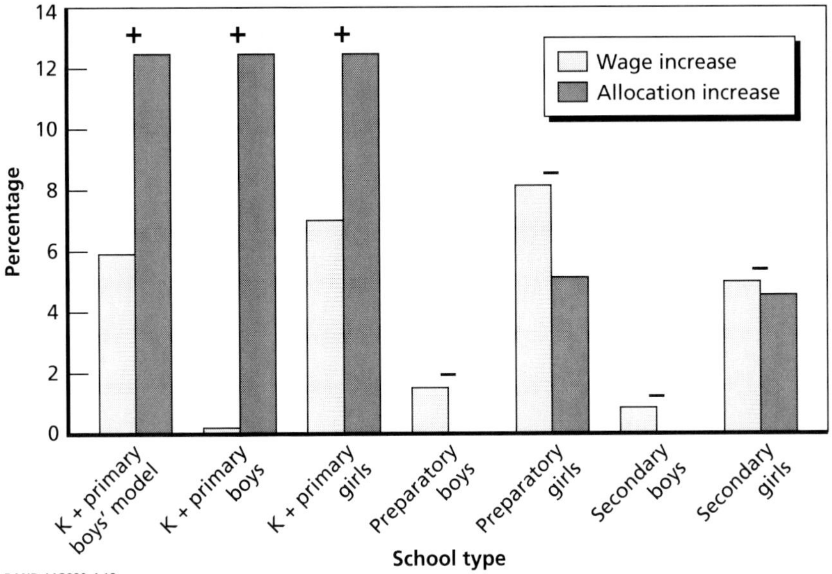


RAND *MG839-4.12*

## Summary/Conclusions

We developed a model to forecast spending in the Qatar K–12 reform consisting of four parts: (1) total expenditures on the reform, based on contract costs, asset procurement costs, Institute costs, and Independent school operating revenues, (2) total costs for contracts, asset procurement, and the institutes, (3) total school operating revenues, and (4) per-pupil allocations for each type of Independent school. At each stage of use of the model, a set of inputs can be varied to determine the effect of various policies. Some of the policy levers that can be manipulated at different points in time to produce different cost scenarios are the following: number of Independent schools; student enrollment per school; per-pupil allocations; start-up funding and grants per school; growth rates in the variable and fixed costs of contracts, assets, and

**Figure 4.13**
**Percentage Increase in School Expenditures Resulting from Qatarization, by School Type**

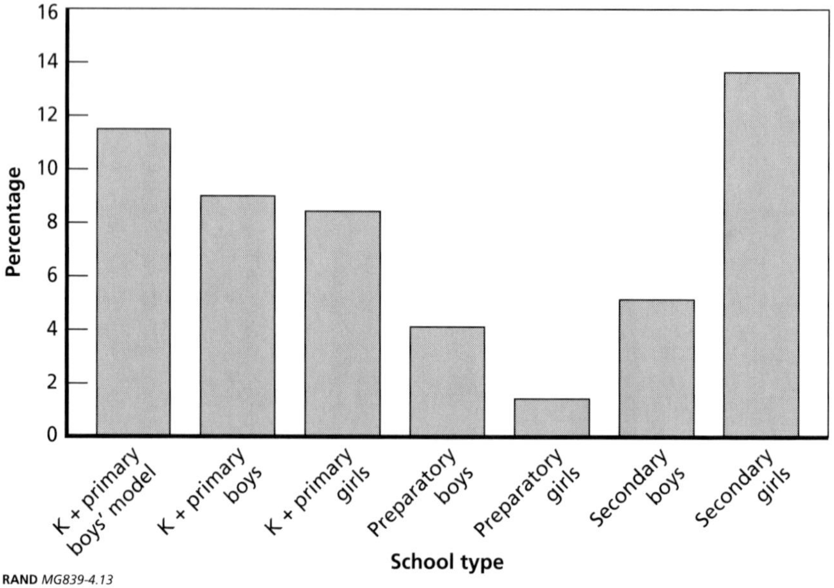


RAND *MG839-4.13*

institutes; teacher-pupil ratios; Qatarization percentages; and staff salaries.

It is important to note that the expenditures on the reform that we are forecasting are accompanied by savings within the Ministry education system. For example, when a school transitions from a Ministry to an Independent school, that school's expenditures are added to the reform but they are subtracted from Ministry expenditures, which we do not track and lack the data to do so. Therefore, from the point of view of the entire Qatar education system, reform expenditures may not result in added overall costs.

For illustrative purposes, we use the forecasting model to predict total reform expenditures under five scenarios corresponding to proposed or impending policy changes. Our findings were as follows:

- Total expenditures increase by 10 percent as a result of a newly mandated 40 percent base salary increase for Qatari personnel in 2006–2007.
- Total expenditures increase by about 12 percent if we assume a 3 percent average annual salary increase for all personnel (above inflation).
- Total expenditures increase by about 5 percent if the Qatarization goals are fully achieved.
- Schools with female teachers have higher percentages of Qatari nationals than schools with male teachers and are affected more by the 40 percent base salary increase. Schools with female teachers can thus expect increases in operating expenditures between 5 percent and 8 percent, compared with increases of between 0 percent and 1.5 percent for schools with male teachers.
- The gender-related effect of Qatarization goals, on the other hand, differs by school level. The increases in operating expenditures due to Qatarization range widely between less than 2 and 14 percent.
- The net effect of the recent 40 percent base salary increase for Qatari staff and of proposed increases in per-pupil allotments represents gains in total revenues for boys' primary schools model and boys' and girls' primary schools (of about 6, 12, and 5 percent, respectively) and losses (indicated by minuses) for boys' and girls' preparatory schools and boys' and girls' secondary schools (of about 2, 3, 1, and 0.5 percent, respectively). Thus, for some schools, the slated increases in per-pupil allotments will most likely not cover the increased expenditures that result from the 40 percent base salary increase for Qatari staff whereas for others they cover expenditures more than sufficiently.

CHAPTER FIVE

# Conclusions and Recommendations

Qatar's K–12 education reform has made notable progress in a few short years. It has founded a growing set of new schools and established a comprehensive infrastructure for financial support and monitoring. In this monograph, we have explored available data to understand the workings of Qatar's education finance reform. We have documented trends in expenditures and funding of the Qatar K–12 education reform, beginning with the planning phase in 2003–2004 and extending through the start-up and operation of Generations I and II Independent schools in 2005–2006. In addition, we have evaluated the reform's finance system by assessing its progress with regard to six objectives: transparency, equity, adequacy, efficiency, accountability, and stability/responsiveness. We have also provided a forecasting model that can be used to determine funding levels and projected expenditures in future years and under various policy scenarios.

We conclude that the finance system supporting Qatar's K–12 school reform is on its way to becoming an effective system but would benefit from a number of improvements. It requires improved transparency with regard to the quality and accessibility of data and the use of standardized categorizations and reporting periods and unique, consistent identifiers for personnel. The partially implemented new management information system will most likely foster transparency if it includes these improvements.

We found that gender parity in school finance is achieved through a tenuous balance that depends on offsetting wage premiums for teacher gender and nationality. Forecasting tools aid in exploring the effects of policies that may shift this balance.

At the time of our data collection, levels of funding appeared adequate to maintain the performance levels of higher-achieving schools. In fact, school operators appeared hesitant to spend all of the funding provided to them and tended to accumulate budget surpluses. Until a more comprehensive determination of "successful" school outcomes can be made, judgments about the adequacy of funding levels remain uncertain. In addition, it is unclear whether the performance levels of higher-achieving schools meet performance levels that are considered "excellent," since school performance standards have not been established. Thus, adequate funding to support educational excellence has yet to be determined. We have outlined a quantitative methodology that can be used to assess school performance as the reform grows, but we also suggest that more qualitative work be done to investigate the resources used in instruction in the more apparently successful schools. In addition, outcomes other than test scores—such as graduation rates, college attendance, or parental satisfaction—might be considered in expanding the definition of successful schools. These can be compared with the test-based measures to determine how well the various measures align.

With regard to accountability, it is unclear whether the mechanisms relied on by the reform have had an effect on school quality. We found that the system is oriented heavily toward monitoring financial decisions made by the schools through restrictions on spending and that these restrictions appear to have had their desired fiscal effects. However, it is possible that the goal of improving school quality might be pursued by loosening rather tightening restrictions on spending, and we therefore recommend carefully monitored moves in this direction. The parental choice mechanism on which the Independent school system—a charter school system—is based is relatively weak in its application because of capacity constraints. This mechanism could therefore be strengthened by increasing the system's ability to accept new students.

In the years of the reform that we studied, the balance between stability and responsiveness in the finance system tilted heavily toward the latter. Many policy changes have occurred in the direction of greater financial regulation. This may be an inevitable feature of a new reform. However, the degree of predictability that would have enabled school operators to establish both long- and short-term strategies for improving their schools was lacking in the period we examined. As the reform develops, it will require greater stability to allow school operators to organize their efforts around a consistent set of policies and expected fiscal and academic outcomes.

The Qatar K–12 education reform is expanding quickly as the conversion of existing schools to Independent schools continues at a rapid pace. Over time, increased quality and efficiency within the education system can be aided through the types of improvements to the finance system that we have discussed in this monograph. As the number of schools and students affected by the reform grows, more weight can be placed on information provided by the types of analyses we have outlined. Greater transparency, combined with this growth, will permit a thorough understanding of the operations adopted in successful schools and the level of funding that would adequately support success throughout the system.

Our assessment revealed areas for improvement in the finance system to enrich its capacity to support the reform and its overall mission. We offer the following recommendations:

- To determine levels of funding adequate to support educational excellence, we recommend continued analysis using a successful schools approach along the lines of the one described and implemented in this study. As the reform expands and performance targets that represent excellence in achievement are established, this methodology will yield increasingly useful information.
- To obtain information that would lead to greater efficiency in school operations, we recommend supplementing the quantitative analyses described in this monograph with a case study approach to examine the operations and teaching practices of successful schools and uncover factors that might yield high achievement at the lowest cost.

- To address potential equity issues, we recommend that policies with different effects on different types of schools be investigated before they are implemented by using a forecasting model such as the one we have developed.
- To improve transparency, we recommend that the new information system include improved longitudinal tracking mechanisms as well as introduce more uniform categorization of personnel and expenditures.
- To strengthen accountability for school quality, we recommend an expansion of the choice mechanism through increases in capacity where possible to strengthen the system's ability to hold schools accountable for providing high-quality instruction.
- To improve stability, we recommend that in going forward, the pace of policy change be slowed to allow school operators to assess long-term prospects and plan for multiyear investments in resources that may improve educational quality. To this end, we recommend that changes in funding regulations be made less frequently and with ample forewarning. A policy of regulatory stability extending beyond one year would help accomplish this. Allowing surpluses to be carried over across years to pay for large expenses is particularly important.

This report has highlighted lessons learned with respect to resource allocation and financial support mechanisms in the first few years of K–12 education reform in Qatar. It has presented and applied a methodology for evaluating the school finance system developed to support the reform. The Qatar experience provides useful lessons that can be applied in other countries—particularly those embarking on ambitious educational restructuring and those in the Gulf region facing similar contextual challenges—and our analytic strategy for assessing the performance of a school finance system can be applied to school systems in many nations.

APPENDIX A

# Description of Data Sources

## Description of Data from the Office of Shared Services

Information from the Office of Shared Services can be grouped into the following categories:

- budgeted versus spent versus in reserve (overall and by institute or department)
- itemized spending by institute and department
- payments made to external contractors.[1]

A summary of data received from the Office of Shared Services is provided in Table A.1. The data include information on external contracts expenditures, asset purchases, funding allocations to schools, and operational expenses of the institutes. These categories cover the bulk of the total spending on the Qatar K–12 reform.

The Office of Shared Services data varied considerably in format, detail, and quality. We received most of the information in Microsoft Excel format, with some limited information in Microsoft Word (.doc), and received data from April 2003 up to November 2006. We based our analysis on the first three fiscal years of data—from April 1, 2003,

---

[1] Although most of the information relates to the education system directly serving Independent schools, external contract expenditures include the national student assessment and school surveys, which pertain to all government-funded schools in Qatar as well as the private Arabic schools. Thus, some of the significant external contract costs of the reform are associated with programs that include most of the students in Qatar's education system, in both the Ministry of Education and Independent schools.

**Table A.1**
**Summary of Data from the Office of Shared Services, by Fiscal Year**

| Fiscal Year | Data Description |
|---|---|
| April 2003–March 2004 | Summary of payments made from Ministry<br>itemized list of payments made by the Ministry of Finance for the Supreme Education Council |
| April 2004–July 2005 | Budget versus actual spending for fiscal year 2004–2005<br>comparison of budgeted amount and spending by category for each institute and department (Education, Evaluation, Higher Education, Communications and Shared Services)<br>Contracts<br>name, start date, and end date of contracts and payments made to external contractors for services provided<br>Spending during fiscal year 2004–2005<br>spending by the Supreme Education Council on the Higher Education Institute, Independent schools, undefined assets procurement, and unallocated projects<br>Spending analysis—budget 2004–2005<br>summary of budgeted and total spending by the Supreme Education Council on institute expenses, Independent schools, contracts, and projects<br>within fiscal year spending is split up into April 4–March 5 and April 5–July 5<br>Technology after editing<br>list of requested, baseline, technology, and actual technology provided to schools<br>Policy manual<br>Shared Services policy and procedures manual |
| August 2005–March 2006 | SEC contracts<br>list of completed and existing contracts by institute and department with start and end dates, value of the contract, and payments made<br>Shared Services Revised Policy and Procedures Manual Spending versus budget fiscal year 2005–2006<br>sum of budgeted, spent, and in reserve by institute and department<br>sum of budgeted, spent, and in reserve, by item category<br>sum of budgeted, spent, and in reserve, by item category and institute and department<br>account credit and debit activity for each Independent school |
| April 2006–March 2007 (up to November 2006) | Spending versus budget<br>SEC spending by institute and department to October 2006<br>SEC spending by institute and department, by category of spending and line item to October 2006<br>Report<br>summary budget report and percentage spent, by institute, as reported on November 30, 2006<br>SEC receipts, payments made, and bank account balance for November |

**Table A.1—continued**

| Fiscal Year | Data Description |
|---|---|
| | comparison of spending versus budgeted versus reserve by institute and department for 2006–2007 |
| | individual institute and department spending versus budgeted versus reserve, by general category for November |
| | summary spending versus budgeted versus reserve, by category and institute for 2006–2007 |
| | individual institute and department budgeted versus spent versus reserve, by detailed item and category for November |
| | individual institute and department monthly (April 6–November 6) spending, by detailed item and category |

to March 31, 2006—and constructed three equal time periods corresponding to the fiscal year to allow for year-to-year comparisons (data adjustments were required, because reporting periods did not always correspond to the fiscal year).[2] We were able to construct aggregate but not always detailed equal time period cost measures, because data-reporting categories changed over time.

## Description of Data from the Finance Office

### Data from Audited Statements, Payments Spreadsheets, and Cash Flow Statements

We received various financial statements on revenues and expenses from the Finance Office. They were as follows:

- *KPMG* and *Deloitte & Touche audited statements*: These contain statements of assets, liabilities, revenues, expenditures, changes in surplus funds, and cash flows.
  - Deloitte & Touche audited statements (reported in October and November 2005) cover the period from September 1,

[2] Cost information is available for the following periods: April 1, 2003, to March 31, 2004; April 1, 2004, to July 15, 2005; April 1, 2005, to July 15, 2005, and July 16, 2005, to March 31, 2006. From this information, we determined expenses for the equal-length periods of April 1, 2003, to March 31, 2004; April 1, 2004, to March 31, 2005; and April 1, 2005, to March 31, 2006.

2004–August 31, 2005 (i.e., the first year of operation for Generation I schools).
  - KPMG audited statements (reported in August–November 2006) cover the periods from September 1, 2004–August 31, 2005, and September 1, 2005–June 30, 2006, for Generation I schools (i.e., the first and second years of operation) and the period September 1, 2005–June 30, 2006, for Generation II schools (i.e., the first year of operation).
- *Finance Office payments data:* These report expenditures on start-up funds, grants, and per-pupil allotments for each school. The period covered is not identified, but the numbers correspond to those in the audited statements for the period from September 1, 2004–August 31, 2005. Similar data were not available for the second year of operations, September 1, 2005–June 30, 2006.
- *Cash flow statements*: These are unaudited monthly and annual cash flow statements of revenues and expenditures provided in a fairly standard format by each school. The data available to us were reported in different months. For example the 2005–2006 data had ending periods of April, May, and June. In addition, not all schools reported in the same manner (some were in Arabic and some in English, some provided cash flow statements with additional categories, some kept to the same original template). Because of these differences, we used only the ratio of administrative to instructional wages, rather than the actual expense, in our analysis. This ratio should be relatively constant over time and thus fairly independent of the period of reporting.

The auditing firm KPMG provides the most recent and most complete reporting for both the September 1, 2004–August 31, 2005, period (or first year of operations) and the September 1, 2005–June 30, 2006 period (or second year of operations) for both the Generation I and Generation II schools. Deloitte & Touche, on the other hand, report only on the first year of operations for Generation I Independent schools. KPMG and Deloitte & Touche reporting on the first year of operation of Generation I schools is largely the same, with the exception of a small number of corrections made by KPMG to the original Deloitte & Touche reporting.

For consistency in reporting on the two separate time periods and because KPMG provides the more recent reporting, we use the KPMG audited statements in our analysis. For Generation I schools, these statements cover both the first and second years of operations (2004–2006), and for the Generation II schools they cover the first year of operations (2005–2006).[3]

To compute a value of total revenues that best serves the needs of our analysis, we adjust the KPMG audited statements data for any deferred revenue related to capital expenditures[4] in such a way that revenues are recognized in the fiscal year when expenditures were made rather than allowing for revenues to be recognized as equipment depreciates. We do this for the following reasons:

- The correction for deferred revenue provides results that are more in line with actual payments made by the Finance Office and received by the schools for the given periods.
- All deferred revenue is recognized by KPMG at the end of 2006 for every Generation I and Generation II Independent school because of termination of the Independent School Operating Agreement (ISOA) at the end of 2006. In other words, as a result

---

[3] We assumed that the period from September 1, 2005, to June 30, 2006, represented the full year of operations for the second year (2005–2006), i.e., the period was equivalent to the full year from September 1, 2004, to August 31, 2005, for the first year of operations (2004–2005). In addition to correcting start-up funds and grants for deferred revenue, we make two additional corrections to miscellaneous income for funds left over from previous operation (one correction of QR 147,435 for one school and QR 7,392 for another). These corrections were made because these funds are not part of the operational years under consideration and are thus not representative of the operation.

[4] We do allow for the deferral of "miscellaneous income received from the students" for one school, in the amount of QR 163,160, and the deferral of "deferred rent" for another school, in the amount of QR 40,000, both in the September 1, 2004–August 31, 2005, operational year. These are the only two instances in which we allow an amount to be deferred because these revenue categories do not relate to income recognition from depreciation associated with a capital expenditure. Miscellaneous income received from students or from deferred rent is an example of a type of advance payment that should be deferred.

of the termination of the ISOAs, both years are treated unevenly; we correct for this by correcting for deferred revenue.

The corrections for deferred revenues affect Generation I schools only and reduce operating revenues by less than 1 percent and operating surpluses by 7.5 percent for 2004–2005 and 7.8 percent for 2005–2006.

### Description of Staffing Reports

Staffing Reports are reports that Independent schools are required to submit quarterly to the Finance Office. They list the names, identification numbers, nationalities, salaries, full-time equivalence, subject/title (i.e., job title and, if applicable, subject taught), and start date of all personnel. Some schools modified or added to these categories in their reports.

The reports we received from the Finance Office covered three academic years corresponding to the first three years of operations of Independent schools: 2004–2005 (Generation I), 2005–2006 (Generations I and II), and 2006–2007 (Generations I, II, and III). Reports were provided primarily in Microsoft Excel format by the Finance Office, and these were then processed before importing into STATA (a statistical software package), for analysis.[5] We processed the data as follows. Most of the staffing reports contained information in both English using Latin characters and Arabic using Arabic script. Because STATA does not read Arabic script, we translated the reports into English. Some information, such as the name of the individual, was not translated into Arabic, since it was not used in the analysis. Then, because of the large number of job titles included in the Staffing Reports, we employed a database query method to group individuals into standardized job categories.

There was a considerable amount of variation across years in the availability of data. We received Staffing Reports in 2004–2005,

[5] Some of the 2004–2005 Staffing Reports (Generation I) were provided in Microsoft Word (.doc) format. These reports were provided as tables and thus they were copied and pasted into excel sheets for formatting and eventual inputting into STATA.

2005–2006, and 2006–2007. In some cases, the Staffing Reports were more like payroll reports, describing actual payments made to staff rather than their contracted salaries. For example, the majority of the 2006–2007 reports use a "paid salary" category rather than a "total salary" category, whereas earlier reports used the latter category exclusively. The former category represents total salary after deductions for pensions, absences, and other items, whereas the latter category represents overall monthly salary as specified in the contract for each individual. Therefore, salaries reported in the 2006–2007 reports are not comparable to those reported earlier.

Most of the Staffing Reports were provided to us in both hardcopy and softcopy form. However, the 2005–2006 staffing reports, with the exception of those for four schools, were provided to us only in hard copy form. The 2005–2006 hard copy data were manually entered into electronic form.

A summary of the fields available across the years is provided in Table A.2. As Table A.2 shows, additional data fields were added in subsequent years, and one indicator, full-time status, was dropped. Not all schools reported all the variables listed for the corresponding academic year.

Because the full-time status indicator was dropped after 2004–2005, we assumed in our analysis that all the teachers reported on in the later years are full-time status employees.

## Descriptive Analysis of Staffing Reports

Tables A.3, A.4, and A.5 provide details of the distribution of staff in Independent schools. We can see the substantial increase in the number of staff from around 1,200 in 2004–2005 (Table A.3) to over 3,800 in 2006–2007 (Table A.5).

Figures A.1, A.2, and A.3 provide further information on average teacher salaries, by teacher and school characteristics. In the monograph, we focused on differences in average teacher salaries by gender and nationality. In Figure A.1, we show the differences by school level (primary, preparatory, secondary, and the educational complexes), and in Figure A.2, we highlight average salary differences by level and

**Table A.2**
**Summary of Variables Available, by Academic Year**

| | 2004–2005 | 2005–2006 | 2006–2007 |
|---|---|---|---|
| Personal identification | √ | √ | √ |
| Name | √ | √ | √ |
| Total salary | √ | √ | √ |
| Salary allowances | | √ | √ |
| Full-time status | √ | | |
| Subject/title | √ | √ | √ |
| Citizenship | √ | √ | √ |
| Job starting date | √ | √ | √ |
| Job ending date | | | √ |
| Gender | √ | √ | √ |
| Qualification (earned degree) | | √ | √ |
| Job identification | | | √ |
| Contract status | | √ | √ |
| Lessons per week | | | √ |
| Discrepancy comments | | | √ |

**Table A.3**
**Number of Individuals, by Job Title, 2004–2005**

| Job Title | Number | Percent | Cum. Percent |
|---|---|---|---|
| Administrator | 39 | 3.28 | 3.28 |
| Operator principal | 7 | 0.59 | 3.87 |
| Operator | 4 | 0.34 | 4.21 |
| Other | 227 | 19.09 | 23.30 |
| Principal | 6 | 0.50 | 23.80 |
| Subject head | 37 | 3.11 | 26.91 |
| Teacher | 776 | 65.26 | 92.18 |
| Teacher aide | 69 | 5.80 | 97.98 |
| Vice principal | 24 | 2.02 | 100.00 |
| Total | 1,189 | 100 | |

SOURCE: Office of Finance Staffing Reports.

**Table A.4**
**Number of Individuals, by Job Title, 2005–2006**

| Job Title | Number | Percent | Cum. Percent |
|---|---|---|---|
| Administrator | 165 | 5.84 | 5.84 |
| Assistant | 178 | 6.30 | 12.14 |
| Director | 10 | 0.35 | 12.49 |
| Laborer | 127 | 4.49 | 16.99 |
| Operator principal | 1 | 0.04 | 17.02 |
| Operator | 16 | 0.57 | 17.59 |
| Other | 295 | 10.44 | 28.03 |
| Principal | 31 | 1.10 | 29.12 |
| Specialist | 37 | 1.31 | 30.43 |
| Subject head | 81 | 2.87 | 33.30 |
| Supervisor | 132 | 4.67 | 37.97 |
| Teacher | 1,707 | 60.40 | 98.37 |
| Teacher aide | 2 | 0.07 | 98.44 |
| Vice principal | 44 | 1.56 | 100.00 |
| Total | 2,826 | 100 | |

SOURCE: Office of Finance Staffing Reports.

nationality for school years 2004–2005 and 2005–2006. Figure A.3 shows average teacher salaries by teacher gender and nationality, and across Generations I and II Independent schools.

In Tables A.6, A.7, A.8, and A.9, we provide more detailed information on the distribution of teachers in Independent schools and average salaries by gender, nationality, and type of school (primary, model, preparatory, secondary, and the educational complexes). Tables A.10–A.13 provide the same information but for nonteaching staff.

**Table A.5**
**Number of Individuals, by Job Title, 2006–2007**

| Job Title | Number | Percent | Cum. Percent |
|---|---|---|---|
| Administrator | 260 | 6.82 | 6.82 |
| Assistant | 151 | 3.96 | 10.77 |
| Class manager | 13 | 0.34 | 11.11 |
| Director | 76 | 1.99 | 13.11 |
| Laborer | 307 | 8.05 | 21.15 |
| Other | 335 | 8.78 | 29.93 |
| Principal | 47 | 1.23 | 31.17 |
| Specialist | 34 | 0.89 | 32.06 |
| Subject head | 202 | 5.29 | 37.35 |
| Supervisor | 174 | 4.56 | 41.91 |
| Teacher | 2,181 | 57.17 | 99.08 |
| Teacher aide | 3 | 0.08 | 99.16 |
| Vice principal | 32 | 0.84 | 100.00 |
| Total | 3,815 | 100 | |

SOURCE: Office of Finance Staffing Reports.

**Table A.6**
**Teacher Characteristics, by Category, Boys' Model and Primary Schools, 2005–2006**

| | Boys' Model | | | Boys | | | Girls | | |
|---|---|---|---|---|---|---|---|---|---|
| Category | No. | Percent | Mean Salary (QR) | No. | Percent | Mean Salary (QR) | No. | Percent | Mean Salary (QR) |
| Qatari male | | | | 1 | 2 | 11,000 | | | |
| Non-Qatari male | | | | 42 | 98 | 7,933 | | | |
| Qatari female | 88 | 39 | 8,710 | | | | 250 | 46.8 | 8,956 |
| Non-Qatari female | 140 | 61 | 6,134 | | | | 284 | 53.2 | 6,211 |
| Total | 228 | 100 | | 43 | 100 | | 534 | 100 | |

NOTE: 49 teacher salary observations are missing.

**Figure A.1**
**Average Teacher Salary, by School Type, 2004–2005 and 2005–2006**

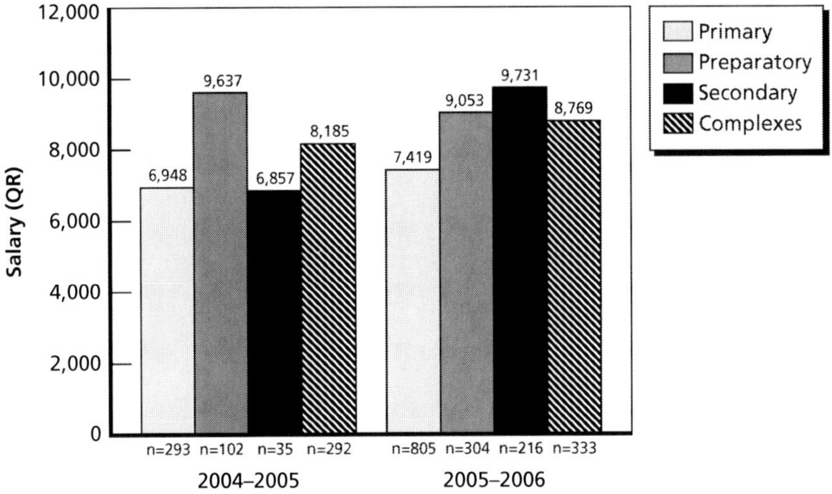


SOURCE: Office of Finance Staffing Reports: staff salaries.
NOTE: Three teacher salary observations are missing for 2004 and 49 teacher salary observations are missing for 2005.
RAND *MG839-A.1*

**Table A.7**
**Teacher Characteristics, by Category, Preparatory Schools, 2005–2006**

| | Boys | | | Girls | | |
|---|---|---|---|---|---|---|
| **Category** | **No.** | **Percent** | **Mean Salary (QR)** | **No.** | **Percent** | **Mean Salary (QR)** |
| Qatari male | 21 | 14.7 | 14,690 | | | |
| Non-Qatari male | 122 | 85.3 | 9,502 | | | |
| Qatari female | | | | 90 | 55.9 | 9,250 |
| Non-Qatari female | | | | 71 | 44.1 | 6,366 |
| Total | 143 | 100.0 | | 161 | 100.0 | |

NOTE: 49 teacher salary observations are missing.

**Figure A.2**
**Average Teacher Salary, by School Type and Teacher Nationality, 2004–2005 and 2005–2006**

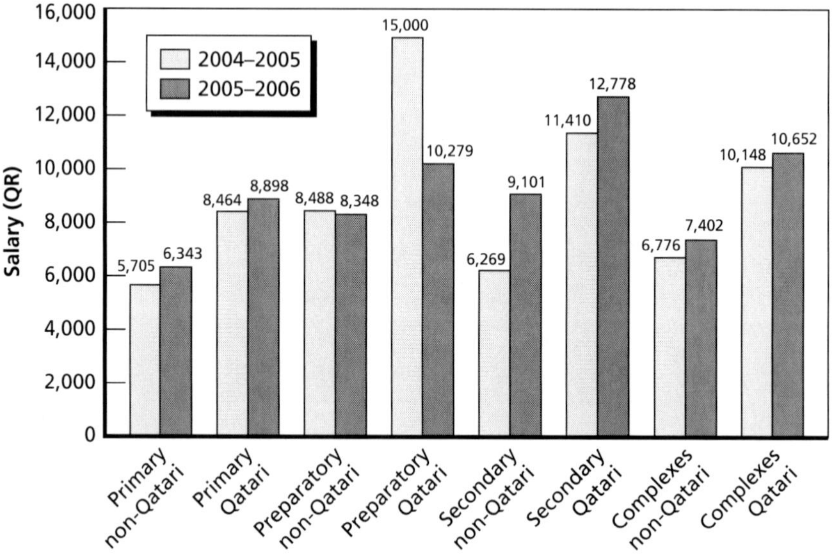


SOURCE: Office of Finance Staffing Reports: staff salaries.
NOTE: Three teacher salary observations are missing for 2004 and 49 teacher salary observations are missing for 2005.
RAND *MG839-A.2*

**Table A.8**
**Teacher Characteristics, by Category, Secondary Schools, 2005–2006**

| | Boys | | | Girls | | |
|---|---|---|---|---|---|---|
| **Category** | **No.** | **Percent** | **Mean Salary (QR)** | **No.** | **Percent** | **Mean Salary (QR)** |
| Qatari male | 10 | 8.0 | 15,602 | | | |
| Non-Qatari male | 115 | 92.0 | 9,982 | | | |
| Qatari female | | | | 27 | 29.7 | 11,732 |
| Non-Qatari female | | | | 64 | 70.3 | 7,518 |
| Total | 125 | 100.0 | | 91 | 100.0 | |

NOTE: 49 teacher salary observations are missing.

**Figure A.3**
**Average Teacher Salary, by Teacher Gender and Nationality and School Generation, 2005–2006**

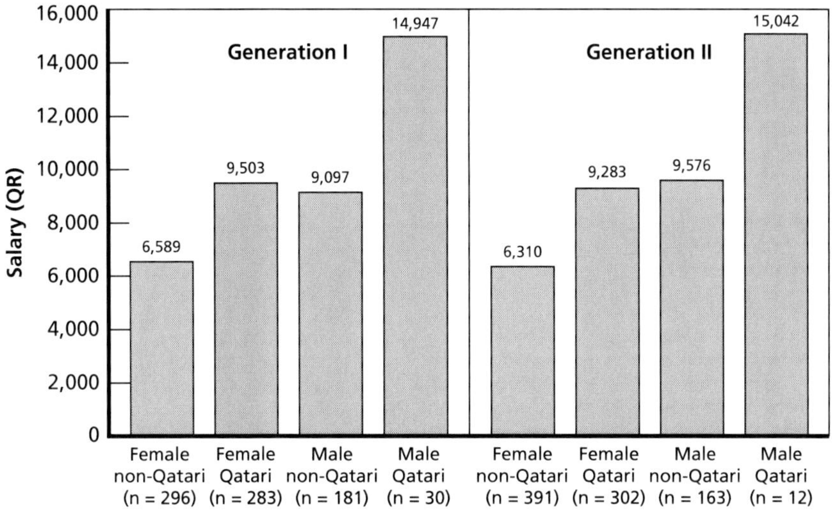


SOURCE: Office of Finance Staffing Reports.
NOTE: 49 teacher salary observations are missing.
**RAND** *MG839-A.3*

**Table A.9**
**Teacher Characteristics, by Category, Complexes, 2005–2006**

| | Boys | | | Girls | | |
|---|---|---|---|---|---|---|
| **Category** | **No.** | **Percent** | **Mean Salary (QR)** | **No.** | **Percent** | **Mean Salary (QR)** |
| Qatari male | 10 | 6.3 | 15,338 | | | |
| Non-Qatari male | 65 | 41.1 | 8,724 | | | |
| Qatari female | 44 | 27.8 | 9,178 | 86 | 49.1 | 10,861 |
| Non-Qatari female | 39 | 24.7 | 5,717 | 89 | 50.9 | 7,176 |
| Total | 158 | 100.0 | | 175 | 100.0 | |

NOTE: 49 teacher salary observations are missing.

**Table A.10**
**Nonteacher Staff Characteristics, by Category, Boys' Model and Primary Schools, 2005–2006**

| | Boys' Model | | | Boys | | | Girls | | |
|---|---|---|---|---|---|---|---|---|---|
| | No. | Percent | Mean Salary (QR) | No. | Percent | Mean | No. | Percent | Mean Salary (QR) |
| Non-Qatari female | 74 | 47 | 4,367 | 0 | | | 125 | 42 | 5,815 |
| Non-Qatari male | 0 | 0 | | 46 | 92 | 5,720 | 11 | 4 | 5,555 |
| Qatari female | 84 | 53 | 8,338 | 0 | 0 | | 156 | 53 | 8,829 |
| Qatari male | 0 | 0 | | 4 | 8 | 23,513 | 5 | 2 | 16,100 |
| Total | 158 | 100 | | 50 | 100 | | 297 | 100 | |

NOTE: 106 observations are missing nationality information, and 44 observations are missing salary information.

**Table A.11**
**Nonteacher Staff Characteristics, by Category, Preparatory Schools, 2005–2006**

| | Boys | | | Girls | | |
|---|---|---|---|---|---|---|
| Category | No. | Percent | Mean Salary (QR) | No. | Percent | Mean Salary (QR) |
| Non-Qatari female | | | | 53 | 40 | 5,117 |
| Non-Qatari male | 32 | 56 | 7,300 | 8 | 6 | 6,900 |
| Qatari female | 4 | 7 | 8,238 | 71 | 53 | 10,078 |
| Qatari male | 21 | 37 | 16,128 | 2 | 1 | 15,000 |
| Total | 57 | 100 | | 134 | 100 | |

NOTE: 106 observations are missing nationality information, and 44 observations are missing salary information.

**Table A.12**
**Nonteacher Staff Characteristics, by Category, Secondary Schools, 2005–2006**

| | Boys | | | Girls | | |
|---|---|---|---|---|---|---|
| **Category** | **No.** | **Percent** | **Mean Salary (QR)** | **No.** | **Percent** | **Mean Salary (QR)** |
| Non-Qatari female | | | | 25 | 44 | 4,610 |
| Non-Qatari male | 53 | 72 | 9,174 | 5 | 9 | 8,500 |
| Qatari female | 1 | 1 | 16,500 | 26 | 46 | 9,542 |
| Qatari male | 20 | 27 | 15,629 | 1 | 2 | 17,000 |
| Total | 74 | 100 | | 57 | 100 | |

NOTE: 106 observations are missing nationality information, and 44 observations are missing salary information.

**Table A.13**
**Nonteacher Staff Characteristics, by Category, Complexes, 2005–2006**

| | Boys | | | Girls | | |
|---|---|---|---|---|---|---|
| **Category** | **No.** | **Percent** | **Mean Salary (QR)** | **No.** | **Percent** | **Mean Salary (QR)** |
| Non-Qatari female | 12 | 15 | 2,633 | 20 | 31 | 6,823 |
| Non-Qatari male | 19 | 24 | 5,732 | 1 | 2 | 12,000 |
| Qatari female | 32 | 41 | 9,731 | 43 | 67 | 13,032 |
| Qatari male | 15 | 19 | 16,840 | | 0 | |
| Total | 78 | 100 | | 64 | 100 | |

NOTE: 106 observations are missing nationality information, and 44 observations are missing salary information.

## Description of Qatar Comprehensive Educational Assessment

The QCEA is a paper-and-pencil assessment battery that consists of multiple-choice and constructed-response questions, based on Qatar's curriculum standards in modern standard Arabic (FusHa), English as a foreign language, mathematics, and science.

The analyses in this monograph use the scale score results of students in Independent schools from the 2005 and 2006 QCEA administrations. Table A.14 shows the scale score ranges for both years.

**Table A.14**
**Lowest and Highest Possible Scale Scores on QCEA, 2005 and 2006**

| | Math | | | Science | |
|---|---|---|---|---|---|
| Grade Level | Lowest | Highest | Grade Level | Lowest | Highest |
| 4 | 350 | 700 | 4 | 350 | 700 |
| 5 | 375 | 725 | 5 | 350 | 725 |
| 6 | 380 | 750 | 6 | 350 | 750 |
| 7 | 385 | 775 | 7 | 350 | 775 |
| 8 | 390 | 800 | 8 | 350 | 800 |
| 9 | 410 | 825 | 9 | 350 | 825 |
| 10 | 550 | 850 | 10 | 525 | 775 |
| 11 | 550 | 875 | 11 | 525 | 800 |

| | Arabic | | | English | |
|---|---|---|---|---|---|
| Grade Level | Lowest | Highest | Grade Level | Lowest | Highest |
| 4 | 190 | 780 | 4 | 385 | 655 |
| 5 | 195 | 830 | 5 | 400 | 670 |
| 6 | 275 | 835 | 6 | 420 | 675 |
| 7 | 277 | 855 | 7 | 430 | 690 |
| 8 | 280 | 857 | 8 | 435 | 695 |
| 9 | 295 | 895 | 9 | 460 | 700 |
| 10 | 330 | 930 | 10 | 465 | 710 |
| 11 | 335 | 935 | 11 | 467 | 715 |

The Arabic and English scale scores are vertically scaled from grades 4 through 11, so that a student's score in grade 4 can be directly compared to that same student's score in grade 11. This allows for direct grade-to-grade comparisons for these two subjects. This was possible because across the grades, the standards for the language subjects have four targeted skills: reading, writing, speaking, and listening. Mathematics and science, however, are not vertically scaled like the language subjects, because the changing topics and subjects covered across the grades do not allow for direct comparisons.

Our analyses compare 2006 student scores in grades 5 through 11 with their 2005 scores in grades 4 through 10. We limited the number of grades in our comparisons, because the two administrations cover different grade ranges. The Evaluation Institute administered the 2005 QCEA to students in grades 1–12 for Arabic, English, and mathematics. Because the science standards for grades 1 through 3 are not based on specific content but instead focus on inquiry skills that are not easily tested via pencil-and-pencil measures, students in those grades were not assessed in science with QCEA tests in 2005. In 2006, students in grades 4–11 took the QCEA tests in all four subjects.

## Description of Qatar National Educational Database System Data

Qatar has embarked on a multiyear effort to improve educational outcomes for all students to more effectively respond to the opportunities of an increasingly competitive global community. As part of this process, Qatar developed a National Education Indicator System that stores information on various education stakeholders. This information is collected annually through enumeration and surveys on every Ministry of Education, Independent school, and private Arabic school. The following describes the data available in QNEDS.

1. school administrator information: school and student characteristics; school resources; admission policies; staffing; and teacher, student, and parent services
2. school principal information: principal education level, skills, and training; professional development experiences; school decisionmaking and structure; views on learning; satisfaction with school environment; and perception on education barriers
3. teacher information: teacher education level, skills, and training; instructional pedagogy used; professional development experiences; satisfaction with school; relationship with colleagues

4. student information: student demographics, schooling experience, attendance and discipline, attitudes about school and education, and participation in school activities
5. parent and household information: parent demographics and education level, home environment and whether it is conducive to learning, child's education background, child's attendance and discipline, parent participation in school activities, and attitude on education
6. social worker information: social worker demographics and education level, role in school, services provided to students, student attendance and discipline, school resources, and relationship with other school staff
7. school facility information: information on the availability of school facilities and physical resources including technology
8. enumeration: information on number of student teachers, classes, and school; track and course enrollment.

APPENDIX B

# Description of Forecasting Tool Baseline Assumptions

The baseline model is the model in which all policy changes as currently proposed are implemented.

## Conversion Period

A seven-year period for complete conversion of all Ministry schools into Independent schools by 2012–2013 is assumed.

## School Types

In the model, we assume a gradual transition over the conversion period during which all Ministry students are moved over to the Independent school system. The total number of students for each type of school, school level, and gender is based on Ministry of Education and Finance Office reporting of the following statistics for 2005–2006 (Tables B.1 and B.2).

## Average Student Population per School, by School Type

From Tables B.1 and B.2, we derive the following average numbers of students per school, by school type for 2005–2006 (Table B.3).

**Table B.1**
**Number of Students in Ministry and Independent Schools, 2005–2006**

| School Type | Ministry | Independent School | Total |
|---|---|---|---|
| Primary model boys | 9,412 | 1,573 | 10,985 |
| Primary boys | 4,103 | 2,491 | 6,594 |
| Primary girls | 13,040 | 6,688 | 19,728 |
| Preparatory boys | 6,610 | 2,511 | 9,121 |
| Preparatory girls | 7,668 | 2,232 | 9,900 |
| Secondary boys | 6,535 | 1,572 | 8,107 |
| Secondary girls | 8,512 | 948 | 9,460 |
| Complexes boys | 0 | 1,860 | 1,860 |
| Complexes girls | 0 | 2,163 | 2,163 |
| Total | 55,880 | 22,038 | 77,918 |

SOURCE: Ministry of Education Finance Office statistics on education for school year 2005–2006.

NOTE: We excluded three specialized boys' schools with 348 students in total.

**Table B.2**
**Number of Ministry and Independent Schools, 2005–2006**

| School Type | Ministry | Independent School | Total |
|---|---|---|---|
| Primary model boys | 26 | 3 | 29 |
| Primary boys | 22 | 4 | 26 |
| Primary girls | 41 | 11 | 52 |
| Preparatory boys | 23 | 4 | 27 |
| Preparatory girls | 25 | 4 | 29 |
| Secondary boys | 16 | 3 | 19 |
| Secondary girls | 22 | 2 | 24 |
| Complexes boys | 0 | 1 | 1 |
| Complexes girls | 0 | 1 | 1 |
| Total | 175 | 33 | 208 |

SOURCE: Ministry of Education Finance Office statistics on education for 2005–2006.

NOTE: We excluded three specialized boys' schools with 348 students in total.

**Table B.3**
**Ministry and Independent Schools Average Students per School, 2005–2006**

| School Type | Ministry | Independent School | Total |
|---|---|---|---|
| Primary model boys | 362.0 | 524.3 | 378.8 |
| Primary boys | 186.5 | 622.8 | 253.6 |
| Primary girls | 318.0 | 608.0 | 379.4 |
| Preparatory boys | 287.4 | 627.8 | 337.8 |
| Preparatory girls | 306.7 | 558.0 | 341.4 |
| Secondary boys | 408.4 | 524.0 | 426.7 |
| Secondary girls | 386.9 | 474.0 | 394.2 |
| Complexes boys | — | 1,860.0 | 1,860.0 |
| Complexes girls | — | 2,163.0 | 2,163.0 |
| Total | 319.3 | 667.8 | 374.6 |

SOURCE: Ministry of Education Finance Office statistics on education for 2005–2006.

NOTE: We excluded three specialized boys' schools with 348 students in total.

We model the conversion of approximately 134 Independent schools with an average school size similar to those of Generation I and II schools (numbers are shown in Table B.3). Although there are 178 Ministry and 33 Independent schools in 2005–2006, the total number of Independent schools is smaller after conversion, as the average school size is larger for Independent schools than for Ministry schools. When all Ministry schools have been converted, the total student population equals that of the population of Independent and Ministry schools combined.

## Inflation Rate

The inflation rate is assumed to be 2.5 percent or close to the average inflation rate of 2.4 percent over the period 1982–2005 (according to Qatar Central Bank).

## Population Growth

Census forecasts of the Qatari population by age group[1] have been used to forecast the population of kindergarten, primary, preparatory, and secondary school populations.

For comparison, historic growth of the Ministry student population was 0.7 percent per year, on average, for 1994–1995 until 2004–2005; the population growth was 0.8 percent and 2.5 percent per year, on average, for the age categories 5–9 and 10–14 years, respectively, for 1995 until 2005 (according to Census statistics).

## Per-Pupil Allotments

Per-pupil allotments are assumed to grow in line with the expected effect on expenditures resulting from salary increases and Qatarization.

We assumed the following wage increases:

- a 40 percent wage increase for both male and female Qatari teachers in 2006–2007, and subsequent salary increases of 3 percent per year (above inflation)
- salary increases of 3 percent per annum (above inflation) for non-Qatari teachers.

We assumed that the following Qatarization goals are reached by the end of the forecasting period (ten years):

- boys' primary model schools—70 percent
- primary schools—30 percent for boys' and 70 percent for girls' schools
- preparatory schools—25 percent for boys' and 60 percent for girls' schools
- secondary schools—20 percent for boys' and 60 percent for girls' schools.

[1] U.S. Census Bureau, *International Data Base (IDB),* undated.

The forecast of per-pupil allocations was calibrated using Staffing Report data for 2005–2006 to determine the percentage of teachers and their average salaries by nationality and gender for each school level and school gender (boys' versus girls' schools). These data can be found in Appendix A.

## Start-Up Funds

Start-up funds are included for Generation I and Generation II schools only, as they were discontinued for Generation III and subsequent generations.

## Operating Grants

Operating grants are assumed to fall in proportion to the number of schools. The rationale for this is that in 2005–2006 the majority of spending on operating grants was related to one school only, a secondary school with a technology intensive curriculum. Further, the SEC has discontinued the use of operating grants in funding the Independent schools beginning 2005–2006. In other words, we assumed that the secondary school with a technology intensive curriculum will continue to be funded through operating grants, but that no other schools will receive operating grants in the future.

## Miscellaneous Income

Although this is a source of income to Independent schools, it is not a source of expenses to the SEC and is therefore not included in the model.

## Fixed and Variable Costs

Costs are separated into variable costs—those that vary with the number of schools or the number of students—and fixed costs—those that do not.

To calibrate the model, we use information on the costs of operations, institutes, assets, and contracts shown in Table B.4 as our starting point. The costs of institutes, assets, and contracts is available for April 1, 2004, to March 31, 2005, and for April 1, 2005, to March 31, 2006,[2] from Finance Office data. Information on the cost of operations of Independent schools (including per-pupil funding, start-up funding, and grants, but excluding miscellaneous income), is available from KPMG and Deloitte & Touche financial statements for September 1, 2004, to August 31, 2005, and September 1, 2005, to June 30, 2006. We have not adjusted for differences in the reported time periods.

**Table B.4**
**Independent Schools Costs of Operations, Institutes, Assets, and Contracts, by Fiscal Year**

| | 2004–2005 (QR) | 2005–2006 (QR) |
|---|---|---|
| Institutes | 34,794,298 | 79,660,096 |
| Assets | 20,518,299 | 29,730,595 |
| Contracts | 273,970,344 | 326,089,366 |
| Independent schools | 176,843,168 | 404,275,528 |
| Total | 525,835,054 | 842,099,577 |

SOURCES: Finance Office; KPMG; Deloitte & Touche.

NOTES: The table presents cost for all institutes. We reduce institute costs by 16 percent in the forecasting model to remove costs associated with the Higher Education Institute.

---

[2] Cost information is available for April 1, 2004, to July 15, 2005; April 1, 2005, to July 15, 2005; and for July 16, 2005, to March 31, 2006. From this information, we determined the expenses for the equal-length periods of April 1, 2004, to March 31, 2005; and April 1, 2005, to March 31, 2006.

# References

Armstrong, J. Scott, ed. (2001). "Principles of Forecasting." Springer Science+Business Media, LLC. New York, N.Y.: J. Scott Armstrong.

Augenblick, John G., John L. Myers, and Amy B. Anderson (1997). "Equity and Adequacy in School Funding." *The Future of Children–Financing Schools* 7(3):63–78.

Brewer, Dominic J., Catherine H. Augustine, Gail Zellman, Gery Ryan, Charles A. Goldman, Cathleen Stasz, and Louay Constant (2007). *Education for a New Era: Design and Implementation of K–12 Education Reform in Qatar.* Santa Monica, Calif.: RAND Corporation, MG-548-QATAR. As of December 8, 2008: http://www.rand.org/pubs/monographs/MG548/

Cheng, Y. C. (1993). "Conceptualization and Measurement of School Effectiveness: An Organizational Perspective." Paper presented at AERA annual meeting, Atlanta, Ga.

Coombs, P. H. (1970). *What Is Education Planning?* International Institute of Education Planning, Paris: UNESCO.

Education Institute (2004). *Finance Handbook.* Doha, Qatar. March 23, 2004. As of June 29, 2007:
http://www.english.education.gov.qa

——— (2005). "Qatarization," Memorandum to Operators. October 19.

Gonzalez, Gabriella C., Lynn A. Karoly, Louay Constant, Hanine Salem, and Charles A. Goldman (2008). *Facing Human Capital Challenges of the 21st Century: Education and Labor Market Initiatives in Lebanon, Oman, Qatar, and the United Arab Emirates.* Santa Monica, Calif.: RAND Corporation, MG-786-RC. As of December 8, 2008:
http://www.rand.org/pubs/monographs/MG786/

Gronberg, Timothy J., Dennis W. Jansen, Lori L. Taylor, and Kevin Booker (2004). "School Outcomes and School Costs: The Cost Function Approach." College Station, Tex.: Texas A&M University. As of December 16, 2008: http://www.schoolfunding.info/states/tx/march4%20cost%20study.pdf

Guthrie, James W., and Matthew G. Springer (2007). "Courtroom Alchemy: Adequacy Advocates Turn Guesstimates into Gold." *Education Next,* Winter.

Hanushek, Eric A. (2003). "The Failure of Input-Based Schooling Policies." *The Economic Journal.* 113(485):F64–F98.

——— (2006). "Science Violated: Spending Projections and the "Costing Out" of an Adequate Education." In Eric A. Hanushek, ed., *Courting Failure: How School Finance Lawsuits Exploit Judges' Good Intentions and Harm Our Children.* Stanford, Calif.: Hoover Institution Press.

Hanushek, Eric A., and J. Luque (2003). "Efficiency and Equity in Schools Around the World." *Economics of Education Review* 22(5):481–502.

Imazeki, Jennifer, and Andrew Reschovsky (2005). "Assessing the Use of Econometric Analysis in Estimating Costs of Meeting State Education Accountability Standards: Lessons from Texas." *Peabody Journal of Education* 80(3):96–125.

Marzano, Robert J. (2000). "A New Era of School Reform: Going Where the Research Takes Us." Aurora, Colo.: Mid-continent Research for Education and Learning. As of December 15, 2008:
http://www.mcrel.org/PDF/SchoolImprovementReform/5002RR_NewEraSchoolReform.pdf

Ministry of Education (2005). "Annual Statistics Report 2004–2005." Doha, Qatar.

Organization of the Petroleum Exporting Countries (OPEC) (2008). "Qatar facts and figures (ASB 2007)." As of August 25, 2008:
http://www.opec.org/aboutus/member%20countries/qatar.htm

Picus, Lawrence (2000). "Courts Wrestle with a New Approach to Fair and Equitable Funding for Education." School Spending 2000: Adequate Funding, The Business of Education. An Online Anthology from the American School Board Journal. As of December 15, 2008:
http://209.190.242.72/schoolspending/picus.html

Qatar General Secretariat (2008). *Annual Abstract 2008.* As of August 25, 2008:
http://www.qsa.gov.qa/eng/publication/Annabs2008.htm

RAND Education (undated). Web site. As of February 12, 2009:
http://www.rand.org/education/

Scheerens, J., and R. Bosker (1997). *The Foundations of Educational Effectiveness.* New York: Elsevier Science Inc., USA.

Stasz, Cathleen, Eric Eide, Francisco Martorell, Louay Constant, Charles A. Goldman, Joy S. Moini, Vazha Nadareishvili, and Hanine Salem (2007), *Post-Secondary Education in Qatar: Employer Demand, Student Choice, and Options for Policy.* Santa Monica, Calif.: RAND Corporation, MG-644-QATAR. As of

December 8, 2008:
http://www.rand.org/pubs/monographs/MG644/

Supreme Education Council (2005). "New Rules Ensure Rights and Benefits of Qatari Educators." May 4. As of June 29, 2007:
http://www.english.education.gov.qa/section/sec/education_institute/newrules

——— (2006a)."New Policies Correct System's Weaknesses and Support Reform." June 7. As of January 9, 2009:
http://www.english.education.gov.qa/content/resources/detail/3569

——— (2006b)."Changes Underfoot: SEC Alters Rules for School Operators." June 7. As of June 29, 2007:
http://www.english.education.gov.qa/content/resources/detail/3568

——— (2007a). "Admissions Policy." As of June 10, 2007:
http://www.english.education.gov.qa/section/sec/education_institute/admission

———(2007b). "SEC Increases Salaries of Independent School Employees." March 5. As of June 7, 2007:
http://www.english.education.gov.qa/content/resources/detail/4538

——— (2007c). "Guiding Articles for the Personnel Bylaws." As of June 7, 2007:
http://www.english.education.gov.qa/section/sec/education_institute/newrules

——— (2007d). "Independent Schools Budget Is Increased." May 6. As of June 7, 2007:
http://www.english.education.gov.qa/content/resources/detail/4957

——— (undated). Web site (the Arabic version, with a link to the English version). As of February 12, 2009:
www.education.gov.qa

U.S. Census Bureau (undated). *International Data Base (IDB).* As of February 12, 2009:
http://www.census.gov/ipc/www.idbpyr.html